VEGAN

EAT

SMITH& DAUGHTERS

A COOKBOOK
(that happens to be vegan)

Shannon Martinez
& Mo Wyse

Hardie Grant

BOOKS

INTRODUCTION

Becoming a vegan chef was a happy accident. In 2007, after years of working in kitchens, I took a break from being a chef to work behind a bar. One day, the chef at the pub left to run an errand and didn't return. I stepped into the kitchen to help, and I realised this was where I had always belonged. Customers began asking for vegan options, which barely existed in a restaurant environment back then. I challenged myself to deliver a meat-free version of a pub classic – the chicken parmigiana. That chicken parma would change the course of my professional life because it outsold the regular parma three to one and attracted international attention.

It flicked a switch inside me, and I realised there was a whole demographic of people who were not being catered for. I started a vegan stall at the People's Market in Collingwood, Victoria, which soon had lines onto the street. The success of that stall gave me the confidence to open a solely vegan brick-and-mortar restaurant called Smith & Daughters in 2014.

My mission was simple: I wanted to give vegans a non-vegan experience where they could walk into a restaurant with a great atmosphere and order whatever they wanted from the menu. No paranoia, no apologies, no stigma. The restaurant became so popular that, within a year, we launched Smith & Deli. It was originally meant to alleviate some pressure from the restaurant but ended up becoming its own beast. Even omnivores were enjoying Smith & Daughters, and the perception of plant-based dining changed drastically. Vegan food was no longer associated with hemp-wearing activists – it was going mainstream. I was asked to cook at major festivals around the country, appeared on the cover of magazines and on national television. These opportunities allowed me to become the sole owner of the business and gain full creative control. Things were on the up.

And then COVID hit. Melbourne was slapped with one of the harshest lockdowns in the world. Restaurants were unable to offer sit-down dining. We teamed up with local farmers and producers and transformed the business into a grocer, did pop-ups and offered takeaway. It was a hard slog, but we made it through. A few months into lockdown, I was diagnosed with triple-negative breast cancer. I underwent twenty-four rounds of chemotherapy, twenty rounds of radiation and surgery. If it were not for my incredible team and customers, I don't think the restaurant would have survived COVID and cancer. For that, I cannot thank them enough.

As the world reopened, I was offered the opportunity to move the business to a dream location in Collingwood – more than twice the size of the original restaurant and deli put together. I didn't need to compromise anymore. I was able to open the venue I envisioned back in 2014 but didn't yet have the resources to deliver.

To date, I've written three cookbooks, the first of which you are now holding in your hands. The original Smith & Daughters cookbook was released in 2016 and became a bestseller, with 50,000 copies sold. The book's purpose was to empower people to cook our restaurant dishes at home. To this day, the most popular recipes made from it are the sopa seca, roasted jalapeño queso and the chocolate pâté. Writing these cookbooks has inspired me to constantly improve the product we are delivering at Smith & Daughters. Enjoy.

SHANNON MARTINEZ, MAY 2022

HOW IT ALL HAPPENED

MO & SHANNON MEET, AUGUST 2012

I approached Shannon to be a part of the People's Market: an outdoor events space in a vacant parking lot, which was built out of shipping containers and involved food, music, art, market stalls and a bar. I wanted a vegan food offering, so I approached a friend with a vegan café who pointed me in Shannon's direction. Shannon was head chef at The Gasometer Hotel at the time and had made an institution of her vegan options. Shannon's a calculated risk-taker, so she said 'yes', left The Gas and we joined forces. She opened South Soul Food and it became the most popular food container at The People's Market.

ARE WE CRAZY ENOUGH TO OPEN A RESTAURANT? FEBRUARY 2013

At the People's Market we were always the first to arrive, the first to set up and make sure everything was right and proper for the day of trade, and always the last to leave, meticulously locking up and ensuring that the next day was set and ready. There was a mutual recognition that our work ethics were on par. An idea was conceived: we should do a restaurant! From this point forward we met for weekly planning dinners, and became unstoppable.

FINDING 175 BRUNSWICK STREET, NOVEMBER 2013

Shannon found the location by trolling real estate agencies and endless searching. She made an appointment with the leasing agent and called me while I was at my desk producing TV. I made up a fictitious doctor's appointment and off I went. Amazingly enough, it was the site of one of Shannon's first jobs, previously a Spanish restaurant called De Los Santos. This was the very place where Shannon had been told she was just a glorified kitchen hand by fellow kitchen staff. We *had* to take the space. We signed the lease and embraced the thrill of the unknown, armed only with ambition and our life savings.

CONSTRUCTION, JANUARY TO MARCH 2014

The entire place needed an overhaul. It had been left in the very same condition as when it had been operating, since approximately the late '90s, and nothing had been cleaned, updated, repaired or looked after. It was dusty, dirty, and ridden with little unwanted friends. Everything in the kitchen, cellar, bathrooms and bar was gutted and replaced. We had a small army of friends, family and future staff volunteering their time to make this all happen before our opening in March 2014. Ambitious, but totally worth it: we did it all ourselves.

SMITH & DAUGHTERS OPENS, MARCH 2014

We opened the doors to media on 14 March for a First Look Feast, with friends, family and Melbourne journalists and photographers eating and drinking family-style. Everyone rolled out with doughnuts wrapped in napkins in their purses. There was a booked-out grand opening a week later on 21 March 2014. Since then, that dining room has been full night in and out, winter, blazing summer, holidays and 'slow' seasons. We very quickly outgrew our restaurant space and subsequently opened Smith & Deli on 16 June 2015. Smith & Daughters has been featured in every major Australian newspaper as well as on many acclaimed blogs and in print magazines. In 2014 we won the Time Out People's Choice Award, against some very big and well-established restaurants. And after this book, the possibilities are endless.

SHANNON IS NOT VEGAN

That's not the point, is it? But really, it's never been something we've hidden or tried to hide. From day one, we've exclaimed it loudly – it's a point of extreme difference to our peers in the vegan food industry.

Shannon knows she's an asshole for not being vegan. She's smart, she gets it. Not being vegan is a shit thing to do, but not being vegan enables Shannon to do what she does.

She creates from a fully different perspective and provides the most unique product for people who aren't coming from that perspective of what something is 'supposed' to taste like.

There are people who won't come to the restaurant because Shannon's not vegan, but really, that's fine. Shannon's doing a lot more for animals and veganism than someone complaining on the internet about her.

Some customers even get shitty with Shannon. A customer once told her that she doesn't trust anything we do ... like Shannon's got weird meat pellets in her pocket, and she's just sprinkling them around. She doesn't. Don't worry.

There have been so many times when Shannon and I have been out to eat and Shannon, wishing that I could try whatever dish she's eating, has gone straight into her kitchen to sort out how to vegan-ise it.

Thanks to Shannon's ingenuity and direct contact, she's convinced some serious meat eaters that her creations aren't missing anything, least of all the meat.

BOOK NOTES

We don't believe in recipes with a million steps and hours of preparation. This is not that cookbook.

When writing this book, Shannon learned that what she thought was common knowledge was not actually common knowledge. She would explain a cooking method or type out her instructions and it would go straight over my head. Shannon buys cookbooks for inspiration; I buy them for instruction. Shannon gives her fiancé three cookbooks and makes him choose something, then cooks the dish without reading the method. I, on the other hand, take the book to the supermarket to get the right ingredients. I make sure the temperatures are perfect and the plating looks like the photo. This combination has (hopefully) made this book the perfect blend of inspiring images and ideas for those of you with the natural cooking knack, and all the steps for those of you with two left thumbs when it comes to the kitchen.

Our best advice: learn to love how to cook. Start with the easy recipes. Cook one thing for the week. Gain an appreciation for what goes into your body and the work involved. Even if you're time poor, make time for food. If you don't have something in your pantry, buy it. Keep going! Keep cooking!

As far as food goes – this book, these recipes – these are the flavours Shannon grew up with. Some of the recipes are adaptations from her grandmother, the main difference being the absence of meat. These dishes reflect the places Shannon has been, the things she grew up eating and hearing her dad talk about, and the meals her grandfather made for her.

It should also be noted that prior to making this book, Shannon never wrote out her recipes. It's her first time measuring things, ever. Her previous measurements were literally in the following descriptors: 'velociraptors' and 'eagle swoops'. Thankfully, she has always been lucky enough to have staff who are on the same page and know the measurements by heart – it's never precise, but it's always tasty.

Another important thing to mention: our main gripe about typical vegan cooking and cookbooks is the unnecessary over-complication of EVERYTHING. Shannon has always, always said that the best way to cook is to use old-school methods and vegan-ise them, not make complicated theories and methods and use extra ingredients to make a substitute. She believes in focusing on food and flavour and vegetables over knife work, so don't be alarmed at the lack of technical instruction, because good, flavourful food shouldn't be hard. Just make sure to have your music up loud and a comfortable place to eat your meal when you've finished cooking it!

23 TIPS AND FACTS ABOUT THIS BOOK

1. Don't be scared in the kitchen.

2. Don't follow the recipes too carefully.

3. These recipes are for regular cooks. This isn't fancy shit.

4. We believe in you. Remember, if Mo can, you can.

5. If you don't have an ingredient, it doesn't mean you can't make the food in this book. Unless otherwise specified, substitute the missing item with something else, or leave it out. The final product won't suffer over a missing herb.

6. These recipes are portioned for 4 people who have awesome, healthy appetites like us, or 6 moderate eaters (not like us). Also, keep in mind – what's the point of cooking if there aren't leftovers?

7. We designed these recipes to be accessible, both in terms of equipment and ingredients. There's no special equipment required and the majority of ingredients can be bought from your local store, no matter where you're from.

8. Your plating does not have to match our plating. Put the food on your plate however you damn well please.

9. Like your food to be spicy? Use more chilli and the seeds. Don't like it spicy? Use less and leave out the seeds.

10. Buy the best ingredients you can afford. Don't buy the home brand if you don't have to. If you can afford it, try to buy up a notch – the end product will be better for it.

11. Even in the zombie apocalypse, the idea of life without garlic is not acceptable to Shannon. So, make sure to always have it in your pantry, even if it's in a jar. But seriously, use the pre-minced garlic only as your apocalyptic back-up. And don't skimp: if Shannon says one clove, she means one fat clove, or two small ones. Go big.

12. In places where it doesn't matter (e.g. sauces, dressings), pulse ingredients in the food processor to get the job done more quickly. No one will see the pieces. Spend your time where it matters. Find shortcuts to save yourself the time as long as it doesn't affect the outcome or, most importantly, the flavour! P.S. Shannon cheats all the time.

13. A comment on soy milk: Shannon always uses malt-free, sugar-free, non-GMO, organic milk when possible. If not possible, try to get as close as possible.

14. Hot sauce – just use your favourite. Shannon uses whichever bottle her hand hits first.

15. Salt, pepper, oil, hot sauce – please use your own taste buds as your guide. 'To taste' means 'to your taste', so just make your food yum to your own standards. We're not eating it. You are!

16. Sherry vinegar – go to the effort to find it.

17. Parsley – always flat-leaf/Italian, whatever you want to call it. But not curly. It's not the '80s any more.

18. Citrus – what's the point if you don't use the skin? That's where the flavour is! Don't just use the juice, use the zest as well.

19. Herbs – use fresh when possible, even bay leaves. But, again, if not possible, dried will do. Kinda.

20. When a recipe calls for dressings or sauces in a salad or dish, we like lots and lots. But, again, it's a preference thing. Definitely coat your dish, but add more if you want. If you want to be healthy, be light-handed.

21. THIS IS NOT HEALTH FOOD. This has always been our mantra, and will always be something we stick to. Our one motto is: 'good food that happens to be vegan'. That doesn't mean it's healthy. You're cutting out cholesterol by cutting out the animal fats, but you're still deep-frying food, and that's still deep-frying. Duh.

22. If you're passing a food store that isn't on your daily route, stop and pick up the things you can't find at a normal supermarket. You'll be glad you did.

23. Turn the music up and have a good time, cos what's the point otherwise?

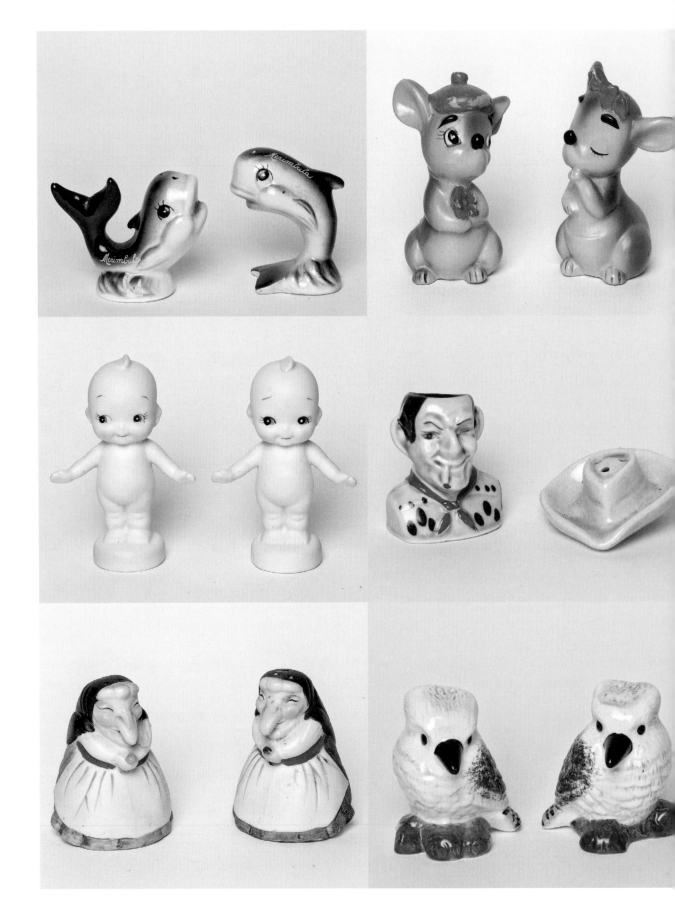

OUR FAVOURITE SUBSTITUTES

Butter – Nuttelex, but any dairy-free margarine can work!

Milk – soy. Our preference is a malt-free, sugar-free, non-GMO organic soy, but use whatever you can get your hands on.

Eggs – no egg or egg replacer. There are also heaps of online tutorials using flax seeds and bananas or similar. Try them out! The world of the vegan egg is rapidly expanding. No Egg just happens to be something we can readily get our hands on here at most natural food stores.

Stock – most supermarkets carry vegan chicken and beef stock.

Cheese – we use BioLife as it's damn tasty and regularly available in mainstream supermarkets, but any vegan cheese you can get your hands on should do the trick.

Prawns – go to an Asian supermarket and do some fun poking around the frozen foods section. You'll be amazed at what meaty/seafoody substitutes are available.

HARD-TO-FINDS

Gluten flour – available from health-food stores. Don't try to use plain flour, it won't work out for you.

Chickpea flour – also called besan, it can be found in health-food stores and Indian supermarkets.

Ajvar – available from Mediterranean supermarkets.

Nutritional yeast – available from health-food stores.

TVP (Textured Vegetable Protein) – available from health-food stores, Asian or Indian supermarkets and often in mainstream supermarkets.

SMITH & DAUGHTERS

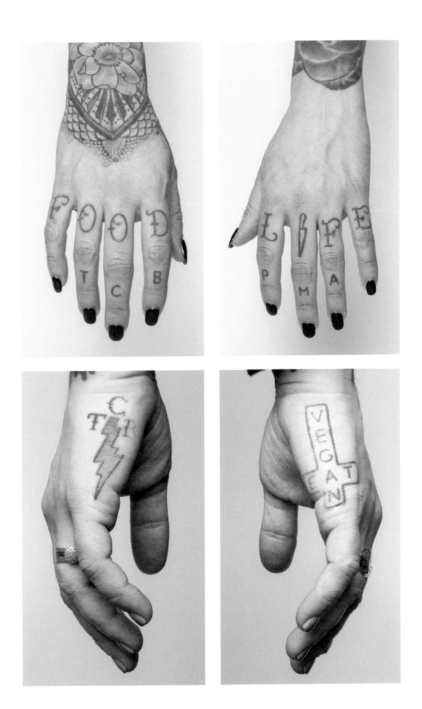

BRUNCH

Brunch is our solution to both of us strongly disliking breakfast. Why do breakfast foods typically have to be so lame, plain, samey, and uneventful? Here's a small collection of our most loved brunch items at Smith & Daughters. We could do a whole book on brunch food, and in this chapter we've included our Brekkie Burrito, one of the all-time, most coveted and favourite items on our menus.

HORCHATA RICE PUDDING

We've served this rice pudding hot and cold at the restaurant, depending on the time of year, and both were equally loved.

Traditionally, this dish is served with poached quinces, but we grill or poach whichever fruits are in season, so feel free to add whatever hot or cold fruit you like.

Serves 4–6

400 g (14 oz/2 cups) white medium-grain rice

1.5 litres (51 fl oz/6 cups) Horchata (page 185)

500 ml (17 fl oz/2 cups) milk of your choice

2 tablespoons brown sugar

2 tablespoons butter

zest of ½ orange or lemon

½ teaspoon vanilla paste or extract

Poached Quinces (page 171)

pinch of mixed spice (optional)

Place the rice, horchata, milk, brown sugar and a pinch of salt in a medium-sized saucepan and bring to the boil.

Reduce the heat to a low simmer and stir fairly constantly for about 20 minutes, until you have a smooth, creamy rice pudding. This can be a little boring so make sure you've got nothing important to do, and maybe a book nearby!

When the rice has cooked through and the liquid is nearly absorbed, add the butter, zest and vanilla paste.

If you prefer a wetter rice pudding, feel free to add an extra splash of milk at the end of the cooking time.

Transfer to serving bowls and top with poached quinces and a drizzle of the quince syrup. Finish with a pinch of mixed spice, if desired.

PANQUEQUES PIQUANTES

Corn & Jalapeño Pancakes

We don't really eat breakfast foods or many sweets – give us a bowl of pho for breakfast any day! But this pancake recipe is the perfect combo of savoury, sweet and spicy. It's everything we love about cornbread, pancakes and the idea that breakfast is the most important meal of the day. But feel free to eat these at any time.

Serves 4–6

150 g (5½ oz/1 cup) plain (all-purpose) flour

75 g (2¾ oz/½ cup) fine polenta

2 tablespoons caster (superfine) sugar

2 teaspoons no egg powder

1 teaspoon baking powder

½ teaspoon bicarbonate of soda (baking soda)

375 ml (12½ fl oz/1½ cups) soy milk

1 tablespoon lemon juice

3 tablespoons melted butter, plus a few knobs, to serve

100 g (3½ oz/½ cup) frozen or fresh corn kernels

½–1 jalapeño, finely chopped (add the whole chilli if you like it spicy!), plus extra thin slices, for garnish

olive oil spray

maple syrup, to serve

coconut bacon (if you can find it; optional)

Place the flour, polenta, sugar, no egg powder, baking powder, bicarbonate of soda and a pinch of salt in a large bowl, and stir well to combine.

In a separate bowl or jug, combine the soy milk, lemon juice and melted butter, and give it a quick stir. Set aside for 1 minute to allow the mixture to thicken.

Create a well in the dry ingredients and pour in the soy milk mixture. Whisk well until the batter is smooth. Fold in the corn and jalapeño.

If you can resist, let the pancake batter sit for at least 30 minutes before cooking.

Heat a large frying pan over medium heat and spray with olive oil. Pour in the batter to whatever size you like and cook until bubbles begin to appear on the surface. Flip and cook for a further 1 minute or until golden on the underside.

Serve with maple syrup and a knob of butter and garnish with a few thin slices of fresh jalapeño. If you can get your hands on some coconut bacon, scatter it over the pancakes, just like we do at the restaurant!

BREAKFAST BURRITO

This brekkie burrito is by far one of our all-time most popular menu items at Smith & Daughters. It's almost a way you can judge someone, really – their burrito-likeability-faction. We love this burrito and love even more that we're unlocking its secret wonders to you and the world, so you can build it to its most personal and perfect ratios. Maybe you've always wished there were more beans? More cashew cheese? Now's your opportunity. Build and enjoy, burrito masters.

To build the Smith & Daughters breakfast burrito, start by laying out your tortilla.

Slap down as much chipotle cashew cheese as you can handle, then top with a big dollop of black beans.

Next, pile on the chorizo and garlic and chilli kale, then top with the tofu scramble.

Fold both ends over the filling, then roll tightly into a burrito – if you've come this far, I'm going to assume you know the shape of a burrito.

If you have built the burrito using all warm ingredients then place your masterpiece straight into a dry frying pan over medium heat and toast on each side until lightly golden.

If your filling ingredients are cold, heat in the microwave for 1–2 minutes before toasting in the frying pan.

SERVE WITH ALL OF YOUR FAVOURITE THINGS:

Guac – as much as you like (page 60)

Salsa – any, ALL! (page 155)

Coriander Cashew Cream – as much as you like (page 151)

Green Apple & Jalapeño Hot Sauce (page 148)

Any other hot sauce

Chocolate sauce (just kidding)

Makes 1

1 large flour tortilla (the bigger, the better)

2 tablespoons Chipotle Cashew Cheese (page 140)

½ cup Brazilian Black Bean Soup (page 66)

½ cup Spicy Ground Chorizo (page 84)

½ cup Garlic & Chilli Kale (page 138)

½ cup Tofu Scramble (page 34)

lime wedges, to serve

033

THE BEST TOFU SCRAMBLE

Forget what you know about tofu. Forget what you know about tofu scramble. Shannon's scramble is award-winning. And what award is that, you say? It's the one our stomachs give out every morning we're fortunate enough to eat this dish. Slap it on toast, add your favourite veg to make it more omeletty, put it in a burrito (page 33) or brekkie tacos, or eat it directly from the pan, whatever way you choose … It's perfect, so enjoy it.

Serves 4–6

Sauce

35 g (1¼ oz/¼ cup) plain (all-purpose) flour

15 g (½ oz/¼ cup) nutritional yeast

¼ teaspoon ground turmeric

¼ teaspoon sweet paprika

½ teaspoon black salt (optional, but worth getting)

250 ml (8½ fl oz/1 cup) soy milk

1 teaspoon dijon mustard

2 tablespoons butter

Scramble

1 tablespoon butter

1 tablespoon olive oil

½ onion, finely chopped

2 garlic cloves, crushed

½ jalapeño, finely chopped (seeds removed for a milder taste)

500 g (1 lb 2 oz) extra-firm tofu, drained and crumbled into biggish chunks

small handful of your favourite herb

To make the sauce, combine the flour, yeast, spices and black salt (if using) in a medium-sized saucepan over medium heat. Slowly add the soy milk, whisking constantly until you have a smooth sauce. Add the mustard and butter and whisk until thick and creamy. Reduce the heat to as low as possible and simmer, whisking often, for 5 minutes. Remove from the heat and set aside while you make the scramble.

Heat the butter and oil in a large non-stick frying pan over high heat. Add the onion and a pinch of salt and cook, stirring occasionally, until golden brown. Toss in the garlic and jalapeño and cook for about 30 seconds.

Add the drained, crumbled tofu and gently stir to coat in the onion mixture. Without stirring, fry the tofu until it browns slightly on one side. If you find that your tofu is letting out too much liquid and it's starting to stew instead of fry, tilt the pan and remove the liquid with a spoon.

Add the reserved sauce and gently fold through the tofu. Be careful not to break up the tofu too much or you'll end up with some kind of weird eggy tofu soup.

Finish with a scattering of your favourite herb and season to your liking.

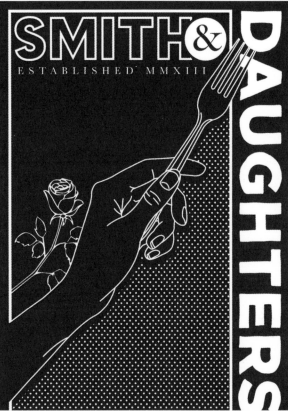

SMALL

In our attempt to make people share, we came up with a whole host of small plates on our menus at S&D. Some call it tapas, and some people frown upon small servings. But we don't see it that way, we love the idea of people getting multiples of these dishes and lots of bread and eating up every bit, soaking up all the oil and juices. The idea of people sharing delicious food is our idea of the best thing ever.

WARM MARINATED OLIVES

Before you write this recipe off, these olives are not 'just olives'. Dare you not to eat the entire pan.

Serves 4–6

1 lemon, thinly sliced

6 garlic cloves, peeled

2 jalapeños (or any chilli you like), halved lengthwise, keeping the stem intact

4 thyme sprigs

1 teaspoon fennel seeds

1 teaspoon coriander seeds

2 fresh bay leaves

1 teaspoon whole black peppercorns

vegetable oil - enough to cover the olives in whatever jar or container you choose

500 g (1 lb 2 oz) large whole green olives (we love using Queen olives, as they are super fleshy and juicy)

Place all of the ingredients except the olives in a medium-sized saucepan over low heat, and cook until small bubbles begin to appear around the lemon and garlic – the oil should be just a little too hot to keep your finger in the pan.

Put the olives in a large clean jar or container and pour over the infused oil along with all the yummy bits.

Seal and set aside in a cool, dry place to let the flavours develop. You could eat the olives the next day, but to really get the most out of them, let them hang out in the infused oil for at least 3 days.

Add the desired amount of olives to an appropriate-sized frying pan or saucepan along with some of the infused oil. Warm through over a low heat, then serve.

Orrrrrrr, to make them way more awesome, add a fresh batch of lemon, garlic, jalapeño and herbs to the pan while heating up the olives. Add as much as you feel works with the amount of olives you have chosen to heat up.

Serve straight away in a beautiful bowl, using some of the infused ingredients for garnish.

PAN CON TOMATE

Catalan Tomato Bread

If there was only one way to eat bread, this should be it. This is a very typical Catalan recipe – it's as if the Spaniards went to Italy, decided that bruschetta was delicious but too hard to eat, so made it an easier way. It's also Shannon's favourite way to eat toast. This is best made in summer when tomatoes are at their ripest.

Finely grate the tomatoes in a bowl. Add the garlic, oil, vinegar and parsley and mix well. Set aside for 30 minutes to allow the flavours to develop. Season to taste, and add a tiny bit of sugar if the tomatoes aren't very ripe.

Slice the sourdough into 3 cm (1¼ in) thick slices, as many as you need. Cook in a chargrill pan over high heat until char lines appear. Alternatively, you can use a toaster, but the flavour won't be quite the same.

Spread the tomato mixture over the bread, then using the back of the spoon, rub it into the bread before serving.

Note: If you're making a big batch of this, put it through a food processor using a grater attachment. If you don't have a grater, use a knife to cut the tomato up, then run your knife back and forth until you have a really mashed-up texture. We've also used a mortar and pestle – any means to get a mashed-up texture will usually work.

Serves 4–6

3 tomatoes

1 tablespoon crushed garlic

60 ml (2 fl oz/¼ cup) extra-virgin olive oil

2 tablespoons sherry vinegar

small handful parsley, chopped

pinch of caster (superfine) sugar (optional)

1 good-quality sourdough loaf

043

HOT CHEDDAR & PICKLED JALAPEÑO DIP

In terms of liquid cheese, this is as good as it gets. This is best eaten when hot or warm, so eat it quickly and with friends who are sad about missing out on cheese. They ain't missing anything here.

Serves 4–6

125 g (4½ oz) butter

1 large garlic clove, crushed

½ teaspoon ground cumin

50 g (1¾ oz/⅓ cup) plain (all-purpose) flour

500 ml (17 fl oz/2 cups) soy milk

2 teaspoons dijon mustard

30 g (1 oz/½ cup) nutritional yeast

300 g (10½ oz/2 cups) shredded cheese

100 g (3½ oz) pickled jalapeños, diced (add more or less depending on how spicy you like it)

80 ml (2½ fl oz/⅓ cup) jalapeño pickle juice

1 teaspoon salt

Melt the butter in a saucepan over medium heat. Add the garlic and ground cumin and cook for 1 minute, until fragrant.

Add the flour and cook, stirring, for a few minutes. Do not allow it to brown.

Slowly add the soy milk and whisk constantly until you have a smooth sauce. If you find a few lumps, keep whisking – it should eventually come together. Add the rest of the ingredients and stir until the cheese is melted. Done!

Serving suggestions

• Eat straight-up in a bowl with tortilla chips.

• Pour over nachos.

• OR, pretend to be healthy and pour over steamed broccoli or cauliflower – whatever makes you feel good about your food decisions.

BLACK OLIVE & DARK CHOCOLATE TAPENADE

The combo of black olives and chocolate couldn't be more perfectly rich and beautiful. We needed another entrée for one of our first winter menus and this was the solution: a dish created purely because we loved the ingredients and thought they would go together perfectly. They do.

Heat the olive oil in a frying pan over low heat. Add the shallot and a pinch of salt and cook, stirring frequently, until soft and slightly golden. Add the sherry vinegar and deglaze the pan.

Add the garlic, herbs, capers and olives and heat through for about 2 minutes to allow the flavours to come together.

Transfer the warm mixture to a blender or food processor and blend. With the motor running, slowly add the chocolate chips, melting them into the mix as you go.

Check the seasoning and adjust if necessary.

Serve with thinly sliced, toasted bread. Or, if you're feeling adventurous, serve it like we do at the restaurant with fennel biscotti, or any biscotti to be honest.

Serves 4–6

60 ml (2 fl oz/¼ cup) olive oil

150 g (5½ oz) shallots, roughly chopped

1 tablespoon sherry vinegar

2 garlic cloves, crushed

1 teaspoon roughly chopped thyme

2 tablespoons roughly chopped parsley

45 g (1½ oz/¼ cup) capers in vinegar, drained

185 g (6½ oz/1 cup) kalamata olives, pitted and roughly chopped

60 g (2 oz) dark chocolate chips

thinly sliced toasted bread or fennel biscotti, to serve

049

WHITE TRUFFLE FOREST MUSHROOM PÂTÉ

Like many of Shannon's customers, I've followed her cooking wherever she went. Admittedly, there was a dark period in my life where I would dress up in different disguises and go to the local pub five times a week so I could sit at the bar and eat this pâté by myself – slowly, because I never wanted it to end. Jokes aside, this dish is what ultimately won me over in terms of Shannon's sorcery. I'd never experienced anything like it. Needless to say, if you had me at gunpoint forcing me to choose, this would be my ultimate favourite dish.

This pâté lasts for ages in the fridge. We recommend saving some for the week ahead and spreading it on absolutely anything (crackers, veg, sandwiches), or mixing in some sour cream for a creamy mushroom dip, or using it as a pasta sauce - it's so versatile!

Serves 4–6

250 g (9 oz) firm tofu, cut into 8 pieces

1 fresh bay leaf

beef stock

60 ml (2 fl oz/¼ cup) olive oil

1 onion, chopped

2 large garlic cloves, crushed

50 g (1¾ oz/½ cup) pecans or walnuts, roughly chopped

15 g (½ oz/½ cup) dried porcini mushrooms, soaked in 125 ml (4 fl oz/½ cup) warm water

440 g (1 lb) button mushrooms, roughly chopped

1 teaspoon thyme leaves, plus extra sprigs, for garnish

60 ml (2 fl oz/¼ cup) Pedro Ximénez sherry (see note)

2 tablespoons soy sauce

1 tablespoon white truffle oil

1 teaspoon sherry vinegar

melted butter, to cover

toasted bread slices, to serve

Place the tofu, bay leaf and enough stock to cover in a large saucepan. Bring to the boil, then reduce the heat and simmer on low for 5 minutes.

Drain the tofu and press with paper towel for about 10 minutes to remove excess liquid.

Heat the oil in a frying pan over medium heat. Add the onion and cook, stirring frequently, until caramelised, about 5 minutes. Add the garlic and pecans, and continue to cook for a further 2 minutes.

Strain the porcini mushrooms and set aside the liquid. Add the porcini and button mushrooms to the pan along with the thyme, cook for a few minutes then deglaze the pan with the PX sherry.

Add 80 ml (2½ fl oz/⅓ cup) of the dried mushroom soaking liquid and cook until completely reduced. Season well with salt and pepper.

Transfer the ingredients to a blender and add the soy sauce, truffle oil and sherry vinegar. Blend until completely smooth.

Fill ramekins nearly to the top with pâté, cover with melted butter and add a thyme sprig.

Set aside in the fridge for at least 2 hours to firm up.

At Smith & Daughters we serve our pâté with slices of toasted baguette.

Note: You can substitute brandy for PX Sherry if you're unable to get your hands on it.

OYSTER MUSHROOM & WHITE BEAN CEVICHE

True story, this is one of the first three dishes we ever dreamed up for the restaurant. We know ceviche is served at mainstream Latin restaurants, but a plant-based one presented some fun. The mushrooms are so fishy and the white beans add a meaty texture, with both pulling out the citrus. It's a beautiful entrée for any occasion.

Place all of the ingredients except the sugar, avocado (if using) and tostones in a large bowl and mix well to combine. Set aside in the fridge to rest for at least 1 hour, to allow the flavours to develop. If you prefer a slightly less acidic finish to the dish, add the optional sugar. We prefer it without.

Spoon the ceviche into short glasses and top with the diced avocado.

Serve with tostones or corn chips.

Serves 4–6

190 g (6½ oz/1 cup) cooked white beans, such as cannellini or any white bean you prefer

1 red onion, thinly sliced

3 tomatoes, seeds removed and thinly sliced into strips

250 g (8½ oz) oyster mushrooms, roughly torn into 1 cm (½ in) strips

juice of 1 orange

juice of 3 limes

large handful coriander (cilantro) leaves, finely chopped

small handful mint, finely chopped

1 tablespoon vegetable oil or light-flavoured olive oil

1 teaspoon of your favourite hot sauce

2 teaspoons salt

1 teaspoon caster (superfine) sugar (optional)

1 avocado, diced (optional)

Tostones (page 54) or corn chips, to serve

+

TOSTONES

This is a more exciting, Latin version of fries. Who's to say what goes with this ... plantain poutine? Go ahead. They literally go with any dressing or sauce in this book. At the restaurant we team them up with Salsa Verde (page 155) and Oyster Mushroom & White Bean Ceviche (page 53).

This is more of a guide rather than a specific recipe. Choose the quantity of plantains according to your heart's desire or the dish they're accompanying.

plaintains

oil, for deep-frying

salt

Peel the plantains and cut into 3 cm (1¼ in) thick slices.

Heat enough oil for deep-frying to 180°C (350°F). The oil is ready when a cube of bread dropped into the oil turns brown in 15 seconds. Add the plantains in batches and fry for approximately 2 minutes until they start to go yellow, but not golden.

Remove the plantains from the oil and drain on paper towel. Keep the oil on the heat.

While the plantains are still warm, use the bottom of a glass or saucer to smash and flatten them a little.

Re-fry the plantains in the oil for a further 2 minutes or until golden and crisp. Drain again on paper towel, then sprinkle generously with salt and serve.

JALAPEÑO & CORN FRITTERS

Moreish as. We serve these in quantities of three or six at the restaurant. People always, ALWAYS choose six. You'll see why!

Blend the defrosted corn, no egg powder, sugar and baking powder in a blender until you have a smooth purée. Transfer the mixture to a bowl.

Add the fresh or extra frozen corn kernels to the purée along with the diced jalapeño and cornflour. Gently stir to combine, then allow the mixture to sit for at least 15 minutes.

Heat enough oil for deep-frying to 170°C (340°F). To check the temperature of the oil, drop in a small spoonful of the batter. If it quickly rises to the surface, then you're good to go.

To cook the fritters, use one soup spoon to scoop up the batter, then use another soup spoon to gently push the mixture off the spoon and into the oil. Make sure there is enough room for them to move around a little in the oil.

The fritters will rise to the surface and begin to turn a golden brown. Flip the fritters over and cook the other side until crisp and golden all over – this should take about 2 minutes.

At the restaurant we serve these with coriander pesto, but feel free to serve them with any aioli or salsa. They're so good, they won't last long anyhow, so make sure you have some dipping sauce ready or people will eat them straight out of the fryer.

Serves 4–6

450 g (1 lb/3 cups) frozen corn kernels, defrosted

1 tablespoon no egg powder

2½ tablespoons sugar

1½ teaspoons baking powder

1 corn cob, kernels stripped, or an extra 75 g (2¾ oz/½ cup) frozen corn kernels

1 jalapeño, finely diced (seeds removed for a milder taste)

3 tablespoons cornflour (cornstarch)

vegetable oil, for deep-frying

Coriander Pesto (page 151) or your favourite dipping sauce

057

FRESH GUACAMOLE

Guacamole is guacamole – it's standard worldwide – but adding mint gives a freshness to it. Avo can be super rich and the mint lifts it a bit. Also, nothing works to keep avos from browning; we've tried everything. Trust us, when you deal with hundreds of dollars' worth of avocados every day, you've tried every old-wives' tale in the book. The only way that kind of works is the plastic wrap trick. But really, the best fix is to just eat it right away. Why talk about keeping it? Shove it in your face.

Mash the avocado flesh in a medium-sized bowl until almost smooth but with still a few chunks in it.

Stir in the remaining ingredients and adjust the seasoning, to taste.

If not eating straight away, cover the surface of the guacamole with plastic wrap to keep oxygen from discolouring the avocado.

Garnish with a few pepitas and mint leaves, and drizzle over a little olive oil. Serve with tortilla chips for the perfect starter, but obviously put this on everything.

Serves 4–6

3 avocados

½ red onion, finely chopped

small handful mint, chopped, plus extra leaves for garnish

small handful coriander (cilantro), chopped

1 teaspoon salt flakes

¼ teaspoon cracked black pepper

juice of 1 lime

1–2 teaspoons of your favourite hot sauce (we prefer to use a green hot sauce)

pepitas (pumpkin seeds), for garnish

olive oil, for drizzling

tortilla chips, to serve

061

PAN-FRIED PEPPERS WITH CRISPY GARLIC

This dish can be made with any kind of pepper: poblanos work well, but you can also make it with run-of-the-mill capsicums. If you're lucky enough to get your hands on traditional padrón peppers, cook them in the exact same way as this recipe for one of the best Spanish recipes of all time.

Serves 4–6

60 ml (2 fl oz/¼ cup) extra-virgin olive oil

2 large garlic cloves, sliced as thinly as possible

4 red bullhorn peppers

4 Hungarian peppers

salt flakes

parsley, sliced as thinly as possible (optional)

Heat the oil in a large frying pan with a lid over low heat.

Add the sliced garlic and cook slowly for about 1 minute until golden brown. (Be careful not to burn the garlic or it will taste bitter and you will need to start again.) Fish out the garlic and set aside for later.

Add the whole peppers (stems and all) and toss through the oil with a large pinch of salt flakes. Cover and cook, without stirring, for about 2 minutes, then turn the peppers over, replace the lid and cook for a further 2 minutes.

Remove the lid and continue to cook until the peppers begin to collapse and become very soft – a little bit of colour on the peppers is totally fine.

Transfer the peppers to a heatproof serving dish and pour over the warm oil directly from the pan. Scatter with the crispy garlic, parsley (if using), and an extra sprinkling of salt flakes.

This dish is best eaten warm or at room temperature (definitely not cold), with loads of bread to soak up all that incredible oil. Olive oil is a superfood, right?

CHARGRILLED CORN WITH CHIPOTLE CREMA & CHEESE DUST

Corn. Crema. Cheese. Duh … this is the most no-brainer, delicious side dish of all time. Add as much of the toppings as you like. (I am not the boss of you!)

To make the cheese dust, toast the sesame seeds in a small saucepan over low heat for 4–5 minutes until light golden brown.

Transfer the sesame seeds and the remaining ingredients to a food processor and pulse until the sesame seeds are almost a powder and everything is well combined.

To prepare the corn, bring a large saucepan of water to the boil and add a small handful of salt.

Blanch the corn in their husks for 2 minutes, then drain. (The blanching process helps to stop the corn drying out and saves you some grill time).

Heat a chargrill pan over high heat or heat a barbecue to high.

Pull back the husks on the corn and remove the stringy silk. Transfer the corn to the pan or barbecue and cook on all sides until toasty chargrill marks appear. Be sure not to overcook the corn as this can dry them out, and no one likes dried-out corn.

Slather the corn with butter, drizzle with chipotle aioli and sprinkle generously with cheese dust. Scatter over the chopped coriander (if using) and serve.

Note: Any leftover cheese dust can be stored in the fridge for up to 2 weeks.

Serves 2–4

4 corn cobs, husks intact

butter, to serve

Chipotle Aioli (page 152), to serve

Cheese Dust (see below), to serve

small handful coriander (cilantro), chopped, for garnish (optional)

Cheese Dust

155 g (5½ oz/1 cup) sesame seeds

20 g (¾ oz/⅓ cup) nutritional yeast

1 tablespoon white miso paste

½ teaspoon garlic powder

1 teaspoon salt

065

SOPA DE FRIJOLES NEGRO

Brazilian Black Bean Soup

Make a big pot of this at the weekend and use it as a base for a million variations throughout the week. Feel free to cook the beans without soaking them first. It works – we do it every day. You can soak them overnight if you want, but all we know is, cooking beans from dry works brilliantly. If there's any tip to cooking them, just don't add salt. Do NOT do it. It makes them hard on the outside and will take longer to cook.

Serves 4–6

440 g (15½ oz/2 cups) dried black beans or 2 x 425 g (15 oz) tins black beans, drained

2 fresh bay leaves

60 ml (2 fl oz/¼ cup) olive oil

1 small onion, chopped

1 jalapeño, diced (seeds removed for a milder taste)

1 green capsicum (bell pepper), finely diced

2–3 garlic cloves, crushed

½ teaspoon salt

½ tablespoon sweet paprika

½ tablespoon ground coriander

½ tablespoon ground cumin

1 teaspoon cumin seeds

½ teaspoon ground black pepper

1 cinnamon stick

½ teaspoon dried oregano

1 litre (34 fl oz/4 cups) chicken stock

125 g (4½ oz/½ cup) Sofrito (page 158) or tinned diced tomatoes

large handful coriander (cilantro), roughly chopped, plus extra, to serve

juice of 1 lime

your favourite hot sauce, to taste

Avocado Cream, to serve (page 151) or ½ avocado, roughly chopped

Pickled Cabbage, to serve (page 136)

tortilla chips, to serve

If using dried beans, place them in a large saucepan and cover with cold water. Add 1 bay leaf and bring the beans to the boil (do NOT add salt at this point). Reduce the heat to medium and simmer for approximately 1 hour until slightly underdone (they should still have some bite to them). Drain and set aside.

Heat the oil in a large saucepan over medium heat and add the onion, jalapeño, capsicum, garlic and salt. Cook, stirring frequently, for a few minutes until the onion begins to soften. Add the spices, oregano and remaining bay leaf and cook for a further 1 minute.

Add the drained cooked or tinned beans to the pan, then pour over the chicken stock and sofrito or tomatoes. Bring to a low simmer and cook until the beans are very soft, approximately 30 minutes.

Transfer half of the soup to a blender and purée until smooth. Pour back into the pan and stir well. For a thinner soup, only blend one-third of the beans, and to use as a burrito or taco filling, blend three-quarters of the beans.

Return to the heat, then add the coriander, lime and hot sauce and cook for a further 5 minutes. Check the seasoning and adjust, if necessary.

Top the soup with the avocado cream or chopped avocado, pickled cabbage and a sprinkling of chopped coriander. Serve with tortilla chips on the side.

CHARGRILLED ASPARAGUS WITH ROMESCO SAUCE & AIOLI

When customers need a good justification for ordering mountains of fried potatoes, meatballs and corn chips with queso dip you give them asparagus! And you chargrill it, and add one of the world's most delicious, complex and rich sauces, romesco, and throw in aioli for good measure. That's what we did here. Everyone loves having that little bit of additional green in front of them to make them feel that much better about themselves. Plus, it's really, really tasty.

Bring a large saucepan of water to the boil and throw in a small handful of salt.

Meanwhile, heat a chargrill pan over high heat or a barbecue to high.

Blanch the asparagus in the boiling water for 1 minute, then drain well, transfer to a bowl and drizzle with enough olive oil to lightly coat. Season, to taste.

Place the asparagus on the chargrill pan or on the barbecue and cook until toasty chargrill marks appear on all sides.

Place a hefty schmear of romesco sauce across a serving plate on the diagonal, then place the asparagus in a bundle across it. Sprinkle over the parsley (if using) and a few sea salt flakes. Serve with the garlic aioli on the side and lemon wedges or a chargrilled lemon half for squeezing over.

Serves 4–6

4 bunches asparagus, woody ends snapped off

olive oil

Smoky Romesco (page 156)

small handful parsley, roughly chopped, for garnish (optional)

sea salt flakes

Garlic Aioli (page 152)

1 lemon, cut into wedges or chargrilled, to serve

069

BIG

Big is better. Music to our ears. These main courses are heroes, staples and dishes you should keep in the fridge all week and share with your neighbours, or freeze for the times you just don't want to cook at all. These are some of Shannon's most special recipes. Some have travelled a great distance and over many generations, but all have been lovingly converted to remove the meat for everyone's enjoyment.

POZOLE

Colombian Hominy & Black Bean Soup

This is a variation of the rich Colombian hominy and black bean soup. On our winter 2015 menu, pozole was by far the staff favourite, although explaining exactly what hominy was to customers was a bit of a task. Fortunately, the staff often just told them to order it and see for themselves! There was never an empty bowl, trust us.

Serves 4–6

4 poblano chillies

2 jalapeños

1 onion, halved, skin left on

3 garlic cloves, peeled

800 g (1 lb 12 oz) tinned tomatillos

150 g (5½ oz) baby spinach

1 teaspoon dried oregano

1 teaspoon ground cumin

½ teaspoon ground allspice

2 litres (68 fl oz/8 cups) chicken stock

400 g (14 oz) tinned black beans

800 g (1 lb 12 oz) tinned hominy, drained and rinsed well

juice of 2 limes

Garnishes (optional)

corn tortillas

vegetable oil, for shallow-frying

oyster mushrooms

olive oil, for shallow-frying

splash of soy sauce

Pickled Cabbage (page 136)

small handful coriander (cilantro) leaves, roughly chopped

Heat a chargrill pan over high heat and grill the poblanos, jalapeños and onion until blackened on all sides. Transfer to a plastic bag or put in a bowl and cover with plastic wrap, and allow to steam and slightly cool before removing the skins.

Put the peeled poblanos, jalapeños, onion and garlic cloves in a blender, along with the tomatillos, spinach, oregano and spices and blend until smooth. Add a little of the chicken stock to the blender if you're having trouble keeping it moving.

Transfer to a large saucepan and add the remaining chicken stock, black beans and hominy. Bring to the boil over high heat, then reduce the heat to a low simmer and cook, uncovered, for 45 minutes.

Add the lime juice and season, to taste.

If making the garnishes, cut corn tortillas into 1 cm (½ in) strips. Coat the bottom of a frying pan with vegetable oil and place over medium heat. Add the tortilla strips in batches and fry for 2–4 minutes until crisp. Drain on paper towel.

Shred a few oyster mushrooms into thin strips and heat a splash of olive oil in a frying pan. Add the mushrooms and fry over high heat for about 2 minutes until golden and beginning to crisp. Finish with a tiny splash of soy sauce.

Garnish each bowl of pozole with the fried tortilla strips, sautéed mushrooms, pickled cabbage and coriander.

SOPA DE TORTILLA

Tortilla Soup

The key to most traditional tortilla soups is chicken – meat, stock, fat, etc. But Shannon's managed to make a perfectly perfect version with plants that tastes just as big, bold and delicious. It's almost like you can never get enough, it's just that good.

Heat the olive oil in a large saucepan over medium heat. Add the capsicum, onion, jalapeño and a large pinch of salt and cook until soft.

Add the garlic, cumin seeds, cinnamon stick, dried chipotle or smoked paprika and cook for around 30 seconds.

Add the tomatoes, stock, corn, beans, herbs, orange peel and lime zest. Stir well to combine and simmer over low heat for 30 minutes.

To finish, remove the bay leaves, cinnamon stick and chipotle chilli (if it hasn't already dissolved) and add the lime juice and fresh coriander. Season with salt and pepper, to taste.

Coat the bottom of a frying pan with vegetable oil and place over medium heat. Add the tortilla strips in batches and fry for 2–4 minutes until crisp. Drain on paper towel.

Divide half of the tortilla strips among the serving bowls and pour the soup over the top.

Top with the remaining tortillas strips and garnish with chopped avocado, sliced radish and a drizzle of coriander cashew cream, if using.

Note: Perhaps don't make this recipe first because you may suffer from not making anything else in the book. This soup is mega addictive and flavourful, and the more it sits in the fridge the better it gets; you will just eat it Monday to Sunday. Promise you'll make other things?

Serves 4–6

60 ml (2 fl oz/¼ cup) olive oil

1 green capsicum (bell pepper), diced

1 onion, chopped

1 jalapeño, finely diced (seeds removed for a milder soup)

2 tablespoons crushed garlic

1 tablespoon cumin seeds

1 cinnamon stick

1 dried chipotle, warmed through over an open flame until soft, split and seeds removed (or substitute 1 teaspoon smoked paprika)

400 g (14 oz) tinned diced tomatoes or freshly chopped tomatoes

2 litres (68 fl oz/8 cups) chicken or vegetable stock

2 corn cobs, kernels stripped

500 g (1 lb 2 oz/3 cups) tinned black beans

1 teaspoon dried oregano

2 fresh bay leaves

2 strips of orange peel

zest and juice of 1 lime

½ bunch coriander (cilantro), chopped

vegetable oil, for shallow-frying

4 corn tortillas, sliced into 1 cm (½ in) strips (this is a good recipe to use up your stale tortillas)

Garnishes

chopped avocado

sliced radish

Coriander Cashew Cream (page 151) (optional)

SOPA SECA

Peruvian Pasta Bake

This amazing Peruvian pasta dish has been the most misunderstood item on the Smith & Daughters menu. The staff still beg us to bring it back. If you don't think of it as spaghetti bolognese, or anything Italian and pasta-y that you're used to, you're in for a real treat. It's totally delicious, spicy and unusual. Make it! See for yourself!

Serves 4–6

60 ml (2 fl oz/¼ cup) extra-virgin olive oil, plus extra for greasing

500 g (1 lb 2 oz) angel hair pasta, broken into 10 cm (4 in) pieces

1½ onions, chopped

5 garlic cloves, crushed

4 chipotles in adobo

600 g (1 lb 5 oz) tinned whole tomatoes

1½ teaspoons ground coriander

1½ teaspoons dried oregano

2 fresh bay leaves

500 ml (17 fl oz/2 cups) chicken stock

400 g (14 oz) tinned black beans (or use whatever beans you have)

Coriander Cashew Cream (page 151), to serve

handful chopped coriander leaves, to serve

Preheat the oven to 170°C (340°F). Lightly grease a 30 cm x 20 cm (12 in x 8 in) ovenproof dish with olive oil.

Heat the extra-virgin olive oil in a large saucepan over medium heat.

Add the pasta and fry for 2–3 minutes until golden brown. Drain on paper towel.

Place the onion, garlic, chipotles, tomatoes, ground coriander and oregano in a blender and process until smooth. Transfer the sauce to a pan with the bay leaves and cook over medium heat for approximately 10 minutes, or until thickened.

Stir in the stock, fried pasta and beans, and season with salt and pepper, to taste.

Bring to the boil, then reduce the heat and simmer gently, uncovered, breaking up the pasta with a spoon, for about 5 minutes.

Remove the bay leaves, then transfer the mixture to the prepared ovenproof dish and cover loosely with foil. Bake for about 20 minutes, until most of the liquid has been absorbed.

Serve, drizzled with coriander cashew cream and coriander leaves scattered over the top.

DTF: DOWN TO FIESTA

We affectionately call these four taco filling recipes DTF – Down to Fiesta. Make them first and foremost to fill your tacos, because you should always have tacos in your life. But secondly, these recipes all lend themselves to meals of their own; great additions to salads, as mains with the addition of rice, or straight from pan to mouth. Use these for anything you darn well please.

CHARGRILLED TOFU ADOBO

There's a big difference between real Mexican food and fake Mexican food. The chillies used in this recipe are the reason why these flavours are authentic. Don't try and substitute these chillies or you'll get the fakes. Search out the ingredients: the flavour of a true adobo sauce is worth it. This is a multi-use marinade – use it on burgers, meats, tofu, anything ... everything.

Serves 4–6

firm tofu, as much as you need

Adobo (see note)

2 red capsicums (bell peppers)

2 jalapeños, or your favourite green chillies

1 garlic bulb, cloves separated

1 red onion, quartered

60 ml (2 fl oz/¼ cup) olive oil

2 dried chipotles, roughly chopped

2 dried guajillo chillies, roughly chopped

2 chipotles in adobo

small handful oregano leaves

1 tablespoon smoked paprika

1 teaspoon ground cumin

1 teaspoon ground coriander

½ teaspoon ground cinnamon

1 tablespoon cumin seeds

80 ml (2½ fl oz/⅓ cup) sherry vinegar

750 ml (25½ fl oz/3 cups) chicken stock

To make the adobo, heat a chargrill pan over high heat. Add the capsicums, jalapeños, garlic and onion and cook until blackened.

Heat the oil in a large saucepan over medium heat. Add the dried chillies and slowly cook off until slightly darkened.

Squeeze the garlic from their skins and roughly chop the grilled vegetables. Add to the pan along with the chipotles in adobo, oregano, spices and sherry vinegar. Cover with the stock and simmer for 1 hour.

Transfer the mixture to a blender and process until smooth. Check the seasoning and adjust if necessary.

Cut the tofu into your desired shape – for tacos, we cut it into finger-sized pieces, but you could also cut it into slabs and use as burgers!

Pour enough marinade over the tofu to cover and set aside for at least 2 hours but preferably overnight.

Heat a chargrill pan over high heat, add the tofu and cook, basting with the marinade, until dark char marks develop on all sides.

Note: This makes approximately 1 litre (34 fl oz/4 cups) of sauce, which sounds like a lot but it lasts for about 2 weeks in the fridge and can be used in many, many ways. And by many, we mean marinate everything in this sauce, fold it through rice for an easy Mexican rice, stir through black beans for burritos, turn it into a dressing, make a pasta sauce with it, use it as a sandwich spread, or slather it on before and after cooking ... go hard. The more sauce the better, we say.

JACKFRUIT CARNITAS

This is a real winner for meat eaters. We're glad jackfruit is having its time in the vegan sun as a meat substitute. It's really special and something Shannon's been using for years to emulate pulled pork and shredded meats. Really, this is what you want to put on a roll with slaw to make a pulled pork sandwich. Just change the flavours around a bit – the 'meat' itself is super versatile.

Combine the dry rub ingredients in a small bowl and set aside.

Rinse the jackfruit under cold water and place in a large bowl. Roughly shred the fruit with your fingers until it resembles shredded meat.

Add the dry rub ingredients and mix well with your hands until the jackfruit is well coated. Cover and set aside in the fridge for at least 1 hour, and up to 24 hours, to allow the flavours to develop.

Heat the olive oil in a large saucepan over medium heat. Add the onion and a pinch of salt and cook, stirring occasionally, until the onion is light golden. Add the garlic and cook for a further 1 minute.

Add the spiced jackfruit along with the remaining ingredients except the coriander. Stir well, then cover and simmer over a very low heat for 30 minutes.

Remove the lid and increase the heat to high. Stirring frequently, cook until the liquid has reduced completely and the jackfruit is beginning to brown and crisp.

Check the seasoning and finish with the chopped coriander.

Serves 4–6

1 kg (2 lb 3 oz) tinned green jackfruit (not the sweet kind!)

2 tablespoons olive oil

1 onion, chopped

3 garlic cloves, crushed

zest and juice of 1 orange

zest and juice of 1 lime

60 ml (2 fl oz/¼ cup) agave syrup

1 fresh bay leaf

1 cinnamon stick

2 chipotles in adobo, roughly chopped

2 tablespoons butter

500 ml (17 fl oz/2 cups) chicken or vegetable stock

handful coriander (cilantro), chopped

Dry Rub

2 teaspoons ground cumin

½ teaspoon cumin seeds

1 teaspoon dried oregano

2 teaspoons sweet paprika

2 teaspoons smoked paprika

1 teaspoon ground coriander

1 teaspoon chilli flakes

½ teaspoon ground cinnamon

1 teaspoon thyme leaves, chopped

2 garlic cloves, crushed

SPICY GROUND
CHORIZO

CHARGRILLED
TOFU ADOBO

JACKFRUIT
CARNITAS

MUSHROOM,
NOPALES & GRILLED
SWEETCORN

SPICY GROUND CHORIZO

This chorizo can be used in so many ways. Fill your empanadas with it or add to absolutely any Mexican or Spanish dish as a perfect meat substitute to literally beef your dishes up a bit. One of our top-selling items at Smith & Daughters was this chorizo recipe tossed with fried potatoes. Simple! And very yum.

Serves 4–6

100 g (3½ oz/1 cup) dark brown TVP (Textured Vegetable Protein)

500 ml (17 fl oz/2 cups) beef or vegetable stock

80 ml (2½ fl oz/⅓ cup) olive oil

1 small onion, finely chopped

2 large garlic cloves, crushed

1 teaspoon chilli flakes

1 tablespoon smoked paprika

2 tablespoons sweet paprika

1 teaspoon fennel seeds

1 teaspoon ground cumin

½ teaspoon ground cinnamon

1 teaspoon dried oregano

1 tablespoon tomato paste (concentrated purée)

125 g (4 oz) tinned or fresh tomatoes, blitzed in a blender

2 tablespoons butter

Place the TVP in a heatproof bowl and cover with 375 ml (12½ fl oz/1½ cups) of the stock. Set aside until the TVP is soft and has absorbed all the liquid.

Heat the olive oil in a saucepan over low heat. Add the onion and cook, stirring occasionally, until the onion is just beginning to brown, then add the garlic and cook for a further 1 minute. Add the spices and oregano, and stir through for about 30 seconds before adding the tomato paste and puréed tomatoes. Stir well and cook for about 5 minutes.

Add the soaked TVP and remaining stock, increase the heat to medium and cook for about 15 minutes, allowing the mixture to slightly stick to the base of the pan to get some crispy bits. Add the butter and stir until melted through.

Season to taste, and remember – chorizo is best on the salty side.

MUSHROOM, NOPALES & GRILLED SWEETCORN

Mushroom haters, don't hate. There's no mushroomy taste in this; they're there to give a meaty texture. This dish is also perfect on its own with rice. But if you're feeling extra ambitious, use it in tamales.

Heat the oil in a frying pan over medium heat. Add the onion, mushroom, poblano chilli or capsicum and a pinch of salt, and cook for approximately 3–5 minutes until soft.

Heat a chargrill pan over high heat and grill the corn until dark char marks appear all over. Remove from the heat and cut the kernels from the cob.

Add the garlic, jalapeño, cumin seeds and oregano to the onion and mushroom mixture, and cook for 1 minute. Add the nopalitos, corn and salt, stir well to combine and cook over low heat for 5 minutes.

Stir through the lime zest and juice and finish with the chopped coriander.

Note: Nopalitos or nopales are cacti. The tender pads of the cactus are cooked and used in the same way as vegetables. They are very tasty and similar in texture to beautifully cooked asparagus crossed with green beans.

Serves 4–6

60 ml (2 fl oz/¼ cup) olive oil

1 medium onion, finely chopped

120 g (4½ oz) mushrooms (use whatever kind you like), diced

½ green poblano chilli or capsicum (bell pepper), finely diced

1 corn cob, husk removed

2 garlic cloves, crushed

1 jalapeño, finely diced

½ tablespoon cumin seeds

½ teaspoon dried oregano

250 g (9 oz/1 cup) nopalitos (from a jar is fine), cut into chunky dice (see note)

1 teaspoon salt

zest and juice of 1 large lime

handful coriander (cilantro), roughly chopped

085

PASTEL DE CHOCLO

Chilean Shepherd's Pie

Simply put, this is a Chilean shepherd's pie and it's how we describe it on the menu. Typically, this dish has big juicy chunks of beef, but we find eggplant (aubergine) is the best substitute as it doesn't have much flavour of its own, and carries all the flavours of the dish while still retaining its shape. This is fantastic served with a green salad dressed with our Lemon and Cumin Vinaigrette (page 149).

Serves 4–6

olive oil

1 large eggplant (aubergine), cut into 2 cm (¾ in) cubes

250 g (9 oz) button mushrooms, quartered

1 onion, finely chopped

3 garlic cloves, crushed

1 jalapeño, finely diced (seeds removed for a milder version)

1 red capsicum (bell pepper), finely chopped

1 tablespoon tomato paste (concentrated purée)

1 teaspoon cumin seeds

1 teaspoon dried oregano

125 g (4½ oz) tinned or fresh tomatoes, diced

1 tablespoon red wine vinegar

200 g (7 oz) firm tofu, diced or crumbled (see note)

125 g (4½ oz) black olives, halved (kalamata is our fave) (see note)

1 tablespoon sweet paprika

1 tablespoon soy sauce

625 ml (21 fl oz/2½ cups) soy milk

250 g (9 oz) butter

375 g (13 oz) creamed corn

1 tablespoon nutritional yeast (optional)

225 g (8 oz) frozen corn kernels

150 g (5½ oz) fine polenta (cornmeal)

sea salt flakes

Coat the bottom of a large ovenproof frying pan with a thin layer of olive oil and place over medium heat. Add the eggplant and cook for 3–4 minutes until soft and slightly golden.

Transfer the eggplant to a bowl and add another swig of oil to the pan. Add the mushrooms, season with salt and pepper and cook for 3–4 minutes until golden. Add the mushroom to the bowl with the eggplant.

Add another swig of oil to the pan and cook the onion, garlic, jalapeño and capsicum with a large pinch of salt. Cook for 3–4 minutes until soft, then add the tomato paste, cumin seeds and oregano, and cook for a further 1 minute over low heat.

Return the eggplant and mushroom to the pan and add the tomato, red wine vinegar, tofu, olives, paprika, soy sauce and 60 ml (2 fl oz/¼ cup) water. Season with salt and pepper and cook over low heat for 15 minutes to allow the flavours to develop. Remove from the heat and throw it all back into the bowl.

Rinse out the pan because you're going to be building the dish in there.

Heat the soy milk and butter in a medium-sized saucepan until it comes to a slow simmer. Add the creamed corn, nutritional yeast (if using) and frozen corn, and stir to combine. Pour in the polenta in a steady stream and whisk until it's all incorporated. The mixture will become very thick so you'll need to swap your whisk for a wooden spoon. Reduce the heat to as low as possible and cook, stirring constantly, for about 5 minutes. Season with salt and pepper, to taste. If you have a cheeky bit of cheese lying around, chuck it in at this stage and stir until melted through.

Preheat the oven to 170°C (340°F). Rub the base and side of the frying pan you've been using with a little olive oil.

Scoop about one-third of the corn mixture into the bottom of the pan and spread out to cover the entire base of the pan. It will be a bit sticky so it's going to be easier if you wet your hands first and then press it down using flat fingers. You can use a wet spoon, but where's the fun in that?!

Pour over the filling and spread out so that the base is completely covered and the top is flat. Now, finish off with the the rest of the corn mix and spread out evenly so there is no filling to be seen.

Bake in the oven for 30–40 minutes, until the top is starting to turn golden and crunchy-looking. Don't let it get too dark though or it will dry out.

Remove from the oven and (if you can help yourself) set aside for about 5 minutes, to allow the crust to firm up a little. Sprinkle over some sea salt flakes before serving.

At the restaurant, we serve these as individual portions in small casserole dishes, but for you, scoop out a generous portion, making sure to get the base, filling and top.

Notes: Tofu – we've had bad tofu experiences too, we get it. This is not one of them. It is purely a textural inclusion as we're replicating boiled eggs that are also typically in this dish.

Olives – if you don't like them, don't include them, but you're a dummy if you don't. What are you, five years old? Grow up.

ALBÓNDIGAS CON PICADA DE ALMENDRA

Spanish Meatballs

This dish goes with mash, rice, roast vegetables, anything…The meatballs can also be frozen – perfect for last-minute dinners, or turn them into burger patties for your next barbecue. Come to think of it, this would also make an epic sandwich filling. Why haven't we thought of this earlier? Italians can't be the only ones with a meatball sub … We serve these at the restaurant over Braised Barley and Peas (page 135) using heaps of extra sauce to coat the meatballs, but you can use this over any side of your choice.

Serves 4–6

Meatballs

200 g (7 oz/1 cup) brown rice

olive oil, for shallow-frying

1 green capsicum (bell pepper), finely diced

1 red capsicum (bell pepper), finely diced

1 onion, finely chopped

2 tablespoons crushed garlic

100 g (3½ oz) instant oats, blitzed in a food processor until they resemble a rough flour

80 g (2¾/½ cup) gluten flour, plus extra if needed

100 g (3½ oz/½ cup) tinned brown lentils

55 g (2 oz/½ cup) chickpea flour (besan)

3 tablespoons soy sauce

1 tablespoon balsamic vinegar

1 teaspoon chilli flakes

1 teaspoon dried oregano

15 g (½ oz/¼ cup) nutritional yeast (optional)

1 teaspoon liquid smoke (optional)

2 teaspoons smoked paprika

¼ teaspoon ground cinnamon

½ teaspoon ground cumin

small handful flat-leaf parsley, finely chopped

small handful basil, finely chopped

1 tablespoon fresh thyme, chopped

olive oil spray, for baking (optional)

Sauce

60 ml (2 fl oz/¼ cup) olive oil

1 onion, finely chopped

2 celery stalks, finely diced

3 tomatoes, finely diced

250 ml (8½ fl oz/1 cup) white wine

2 fresh bay leaves

3 thyme sprigs

handful parsley stalks

1 litre (34 fl oz/4 cups) chicken or vegetable stock

Picada

2 tablespoons extra-virgin olive oil

2 slices sourdough or white bread, cut into cubes

1 tablespoon crushed garlic

80 g (2¾ oz/½ cup) almonds, toasted

small handful flat-leaf parsley, roughly chopped

1 tablespoon sweet paprika

pinch of saffron

zest of 1 lemon

1 teaspoon chopped thyme

089

ALBÓNDIGAS CON PICADA DE ALMENDRA cont.

To make the meatballs, cook the rice in plenty of salted boiling water over medium heat until almost over-cooked, about 20 minutes. Drain and set aside in a large bowl.

Heat a large glug of oil in a large frying pan over medium heat. Add the capsicum, onion and garlic and cook, stirring occasionally, for about 5 minutes until very soft.

Add the cooked vegetables to the rice along with the remaining ingredients. Season to taste and mix very well. Set aside in the fridge to firm up for at least 1 hour.

Shape the mixture into small balls (ball size is completely personal, but the larger the balls, the longer they will take to cook). If the mixture is a little wet, add 1 tablespoon gluten flour at a time until the balls maintain their shape. Refrigerate until firm.

Heat a nonstick frying pan with plenty of oil and fry the meatballs in batches over medium heat until golden brown all over. Alternatively, you can spray the meatballs with olive oil and cook in a 170°C (340°C) oven on a baking tray lined with baking paper for 20–30 minutes, until golden brown.

To make the sauce, heat the oil in a medium-sized saucepan over low heat. Add the onion, celery and tomato and cook, stirring occasionally, for about 5 minutes until soft. Add the wine and herbs and cook until the wine has reduced by half. Add the stock, increase the temperature to medium and simmer until the sauce has reduced by half.

To make the picada, heat the oil in a small frying pan and fry the bread over medium–high heat until golden on all sides. Transfer to a food processor along with the remaining ingredients and pulse until it forms a rough paste.

Add the meatballs to the sauce to heat through, stirring gently. Remove the meatballs and set aside.

Slowly add the picada to the sauce, stirring constantly over low heat until thickened. Return the meatballs to the pan and coat in the sauce.

Serve with braised barley and peas (like we do at the restaurant), or with rice, mash, roast veg, bread – anthing you want!

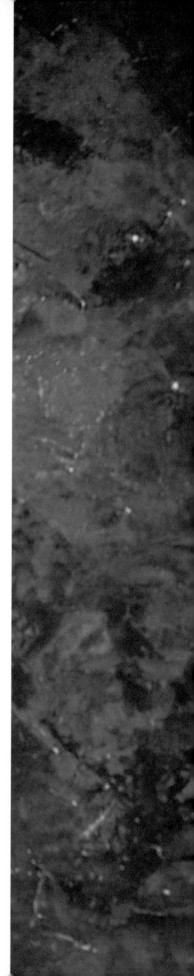

PASTELES DE CANGREJO

Crab Cakes

We know this looks like a hard recipe with a bunch of ingredients at first glance, but it's really not. Give it a go! For parties, make smaller golf ball-sized cakes and dress with mango salsa and avocado cream – they're a really great finger-food option.

Place the potato in a medium-sized saucepan and cover with cold water. Add the bay leaf, whole garlic cloves and salt, then bring to the boil over high heat and reduce to a simmer. Cook until you can easily pierce the potato with a knife. Drain, remove the bay leaf, and transfer the potato and garlic to a large bowl along with 1 tablespoon of the butter. Mash, then season to taste and set aside to cool to room temperature.

Drain the hearts of palm and rinse under cold water. Cut into 2.5 cm (1 in) lengths and shred with your fingers until it resembles crab meat.

Heat the remaining tablespoon of butter in a medium-sized frying pan over medium heat. Add the shredded palm and fry for a few minutes, until it begins to lightly brown. Add the celery, spring onion, jalapeño and crushed garlic. Cook until the vegetables begin to soften, then add the fish sauce, Old Bay Seasoning and ground cumin. Season with salt and pepper, then transfer this mixture to the mash. Add the mustard, dill, coriander and lime zest and stir to combine. Put the mixture in the fridge to cool completely.

Shape the mixture into tennis ball-sized balls (or roll into golf ball-sized balls for a finger-food option). Flatten your balls into thick discs and put back into the fridge for about 30 minutes to firm up.

To prepare the crumb, pour the soy milk into one bowl and add the vinegar. Mix and set aside – it will thicken slightly. Add the flour to another bowl and season to your liking with salt and pepper. Place the panko crumbs in a third bowl.

Coat each crab cake with the flour, then dip into the soy milk wash and finally in the panko breadcrumbs. Make sure they are well coated with no gaps.

Place the crumbed crab cakes back into the fridge so the crumb can set.

Pour vegetable oil in a large frying pan until 1 cm (½ in) deep and place over medium heat. Cook the crab cakes, 3–4 patties at a time, for 3–4 minutes on each side until golden and crunchy. Drain on paper towel and season with salt flakes.

Serve with mango salsa and avocado cream or any aioli dipping sauce that you love.

Notes: If you have the luxury of having access to fake meat, you can substitute crab meat for the hearts of palm – just a tip. Unless you live in the US, you will probably need to buy Old Bay Seasoning online.

Serves 4–6

500 g (1 lb 2 oz) potatoes, peeled and diced

1 fresh bay leaf

4 garlic cloves, 2 peeled, 2 crushed

1 teaspoon fine salt

2 tablespoons butter

425 g (15 oz) tinned hearts of palm (see note)

2 celery stalks, finely diced

2 large spring onions (scallions), thinly sliced

½ jalapeño, seeds removed and finely diced

2 teaspoons fish sauce

1 teaspoon Old Bay Seasoning (see note)

½ teaspoon ground cumin

1 tablespoon dijon mustard

1 tablespoon chopped dill

1 tablespoon chopped coriander (cilantro)

zest of 1 lime

vegetable oil, for shallow-frying

sea salt flakes

Mango Salsa (page 155), Avocado Cream (page 151) or Aioli (page 152), to serve

Crumb

500 ml (17 fl oz/2 cups) soy milk

2 tablespoons apple cider vinegar

150 g (5½ oz/1 cup) plain (all-purpose) flour

200 g (7 oz/2 cups) panko breadcrumbs (use regular breadcrumbs if you can't find panko)

GAMBAS AL AJILLO

Prawns

These garlic prawns were such a hit at the restaurant, our customers protested when they came off the menu for a season. They're so sincerely like prawns that it fools even the most meaty of meat eaters. In truth, we were hesitant to include this recipe as it calls for a mock meat product. We wanted this book to include mostly items you could typically find at your local supermarket, even if you live in the country. But if you're in a place lucky enough to have an Asian supermarket with a faux meat section, or a vegan convenience store, or even have the option of ordering vegan prawns online – do it!

The magic of this recipe is the delicious sauce. The yummy oil is one of the best parts of this dish: garlic, chilli, oil, lemon, yes!

Serves 4–6

125 ml (4 fl oz/½ cup) extra-virgin olive oil

1 kg (2 lb 3 oz) vegan prawns, defrosted if frozen

35 g (1¼ oz/¼ cup) crushed garlic

2 teaspoons smoked paprika

3 bird's eye chillies, thinly sliced (seeds removed for a milder taste)

zest and juice of 2 lemons

½ bunch flat-leaf parsley, roughly chopped

toasted bread, to serve

Heat the oil in a large frying pan over high heat and add the prawns. Cook for a few minutes until the prawns are heated through.

Add the garlic, smoked paprika, chilli and lemon zest and toss through to combine. Cook for a further 1 minute. Add the lemon juice and chopped parsley and toss again. Don't worry if the prawns catch on fire a little bit – it just means you've gone up a level in cheffing!

Season to taste and serve with loads of toasted bread to soak up all that delicious oil.

PAELLA

Sure, you've had paella before, but this happens to be Shan's Gran's fifth (maybe more) generation recipe and the story of the distance it has travelled is really quite amazing. Shannon's family, originally from Andalusia, Spain, responded to an ad on the front page of the local newspaper calling for Europeans to move to Australia – only tradespeople of specific skill need apply. Shannon's granddad studied for two years to become a boilermaker. He graduated just in time as the very last Europeans were allowed to emigrate. They arrived in Darwin, five kids in tow. Now, compared to the luscious Andalusia, it was just red dirt as far as the eye could see, and while the end of this story is what you have here, you can be sure they were thinking 'where are we and what have we done'?! If they knew their descendants would use this well-loved and travelled recipe to make vegan paella, they may have had the same reaction – what have we done?! That being said, you can add anything to this paella – prawns, sausage, squid, seasonal veg. Just cook separately and add to the paella at the end.

Serves 4-6

1.25 litres (42 fl oz/5 cups) chicken or vegetable stock

1 large pinch of saffron threads

60 ml (2 fl oz/¼ cup) olive oil

1 medium onion, chopped

½ green capsicum (bell pepper), diced

½ red capsicum (bell pepper), diced

1 teaspoon fine salt

2 tomatoes, tinned or fresh, diced (only use fresh if tomatoes are in season)

3 garlic cloves, crushed

2 teaspoons sweet paprika

1 teaspoon smoked paprika

400 g (14 oz) bomba or medium-grain rice

185 g (6½ oz) podded broad (fava) beans or substitute peas

cooked seasonal veg, such as asparagus and peas in spring or pumpkin (squash) and olives in winter (see note)

Garnish

lemons, cut into wedges

extra-virgin olive oil

sea salt flakes

flat-leaf parsley, roughly chopped

Place the stock in a medium-sized saucepan and bring to the boil. Remove from the heat and drop in the saffron. Set aside to infuse for at least 5 minutes. You will see the stock turn bright yellow.

Heat the oil in a 30 cm (12 in) – or slightly larger – paella pan or ovenproof casserole dish over low heat. Add the onion, capsicum and salt and cook, stirring occasionally, for about 15 minutes, until the vegetables are very soft and almost jammy. Add the tomato and garlic and cook for a further 15 minutes or until the sauce becomes thick. If you have pre-made Sofrito (page 159) handy, use 250 g (9 oz/1 cup) of this instead.

Add the paprikas and stir to combine, then add the rice and broad beans and coat with the sauce. Cook for 1–2 minutes, or until the rice begins to turn translucent.

Preheat the oven to 150°C (300°F).

Pour the stock over the rice and turn up the heat to high. Stir to make sure the rice is evenly spread across the pan, then simmer for exactly 5 minutes. Do not stir.

Transfer the paella to the oven and cook for 12–15 minutes until the liquid has been absorbed.

Remove from the oven and stir through the cooked seasonal veg. Cover the pan with a clean tea towel and set aside for 5 minutes.

Place lemon wedges sporadically but evenly throughout the paella, drizzle with extra-virgin olive oil and sprinkle with sea salt flakes and chopped parsley.

KALE & LEEK BAKE

It's not like we're trying, but we've struggled to find anyone who doesn't love this dish. The cream sauce, the kale, the garlic breadcrumbs on top ... It's literally the most perfect creamy casserole-style dish that will inspire second and third helpings.

Pour the soy milk and stock in a medium-sized saucepan and add the onion, smashed garlic, fennel seeds, bay leaves, peppercorns, parsley stalks and green leek ends. Bring to the boil, then remove from the heat and allow to infuse for 15 minutes. Strain the liquid into a bowl and discard the leftover ingredients.

Heat 1 tablespoon of the butter and a glug of olive oil in a saucepan over medium heat. Add the chopped leek with a pinch of salt and cook until soft but not coloured. Remove from the pan and set aside in a small bowl.

Bring a large saucepan of water to the boil and throw in a large pinch of salt. Drop in the kale leaves and boil for 3–4 minutes or until the leaves have begun to soften but still have their bright green colour. Drain and refresh under cold running water until the leaves are cool. This will stop the cooking process.

Preheat the oven to 180°C (350°F). Grease four individual or one large ovenproof dish with a little butter.

Heat the remaining butter in a medium-sized saucepan over low heat until melted. Add half of the crushed garlic and the thyme and cook for about 30 seconds before adding the flour. Stir well to combine and cook until it becomes a thick paste. Cook over low heat for about 1 minute to cook out the raw flour, then slowly add the strained infused soy milk, stirring constantly to keep the sauce smooth. Add the shredded cheese and mustard and continue to stir over a low heat until the cheese has melted. Season with salt and pepper.

Either tear the bread into small pieces or pulse in a food processor until you have chunky breadcrumbs. Heat a frying pan over medium heat and add a big glug of olive oil. Add the remaining crushed garlic, the chopped parsley and the breadcrumbs along with a pinch of salt and toss well to coat in the oil. Cook over medium heat tossing often until the breadcrumbs are just beginning to turn a light golden brown. Remove from the heat and set aside.

Add the kale and leeks to the sauce and stir until evenly combined. Pour into the prepared ovenproof dish/es and top with the garlicky breadcrumbs.

Bake in the oven for approximately 20 minutes, until golden brown and bubbling.

Serves 4–6

500 ml (17 fl oz/2 cups) soy milk

250 ml (8½ fl oz/1 cup) vegetable stock

½ onion, peeled and halved

3 garlic cloves, 1 smashed, 2 crushed

pinch of fennel seeds

2 fresh bay leaves

pinch of whole black peppercorns

handful chopped flat-leaf parsley, reserving the stalks for the stock

4 large leeks, cut in half lengthways and sliced into 1 cm (½) pieces, reserving the dark green ends for the stock

80 g (2¾ oz) butter, plus extra for greasing

olive oil, for frying

1 large bunch kale, leaves stripped and roughly torn

1 teaspoon finely chopped thyme

35 g (1¼ oz) plain (all-purpose) flour

120 g (4 oz) shredded cheese

1 tablespoon dijon mustard

stale bread

GARBANZOS ESTOFADOS

Chickpea Stew

This is one of those magical Shannon Martinez dishes that is made purely of veg, but still has a very meaty taste and is just as filling (if not more) than a beefy stew. Also, it's a seemingly typical dish to find in a vegan cookbook, but there's definitely something different about the bold, big and juicy flavours of this stew that are typically missing in dishes that don't rely on animal flesh. That's Martinez gold right there.

Serves 4–6

2 tablespoons olive oil

1 large onion, finely chopped

1 large red capsicum (bell pepper), finely diced

2 celery stalks, finely diced

2 garlic cloves, crushed

2 teaspoons sweet paprika

1 teaspoon smoked paprika

½ teaspoon chilli flakes

½ teaspoon dried oregano

1 pinch of saffron threads

400 g (14 oz) tinned whole peeled tomatoes

750 g (1 lb 11 oz) potatoes, peeled and chopped into chunky pieces

400 g (14 oz) carrots, peeled and cut into chunky pieces

400 g (14 oz) cooked or tinned chickpeas, drained and rinsed

350 g (12½ oz) silverbeet (Swiss chard) stalks removed and chopped, leaves sliced

2 fresh bay leaves

small handful thyme

1 litre (34 fl oz/4 cups) chicken or vegetable stock, plus extra if necessary

handful flat-leaf parsley, roughly chopped

crusty bread, to serve

Heat the oil in a large casserole dish over medium heat. Add the onion, capsicum, celery and garlic along with a good pinch of salt. Reduce the heat to low and cook, stirring occasionally, for about 15 minutes or until very soft.

Add both paprikas, chilli flakes, oregano and saffron and cook for 1 minute. Add the tomatoes, breaking them up with a spoon, then cook on the lowest heat for about 20 minutes or until the mixture is thick and jammy.

Add the potato and stir well to coat. Add the carrot, chickpeas, silverbeet stalks, bay leaves and thyme, then pour over the stock. You want to make sure that everything is covered in the liquid so add a little more stock, if necessary. Season with salt and pepper.

Cook over low heat for approximately 1 hour or until the potatoes can be easily pierced with a knife. Add the silverbeet leaves and cook for a further 5 minutes until the leaves are wilted but still bright green. Finish with the chopped parsley and adjust the seasoning, to taste.

Serve with piles of crusty bread. Make sure you or anyone else eating this does not leave any sauce in the bowl.

SHANNON'S PANTRY LIST

tinned tomatoes

organic coconut milk

organic coconut cream

tinned black beans

tinned chickpeas

tinned white beans

refried beans

gravy powder

creamed corn

bamboo shoots

water chestnuts

hot German mustard

hot English mustard

seeded mustard

extra-hot jalapeño mustard

habanero mustard

dijon mustard

American mustard

tomato sauce (ketchup)

chunky peanut butter

Vegemite

Promite

jam (apricot)

custard powder

coconut oil

rice bran oil

vegetable oil

regular olive oil

extra-virgin olive oil

coconut oil spray

vegetable oil spray

olive oil spray

sesame oil (Korean, roasted sesame)

truffle oil

molasses, dark

golden syrup

passata

BBQ sauce

Thai curry paste (all of them)

Malaysian curry paste (all of them)

Japanese golden curry paste

rogan Josh curry paste

rendang curry paste (3 types)

tamarind paste

glutinous rice

Korean rice

brown jasmine rice

regular jasmine rice

black wild rice

bomba rice

medium-grain rice

regular brown rice

basmati rice

long-grain rice

arborio rice

instant ramen soup

instant udon noodle soup

ramen in a bowl

hokkien noodles

flat rice noodles

vermicelli noodles

wholegrain pasta

farro pasta

regular pasta

pasta in every shape

gym pasta (pretend pasta made from mung beans)

couscous

Israeli (pearl) couscous

risoni

short noodles for noodle soups

rice paper sheets

polenta (fine cornmeal)

rice crackers

dried porcini mushrooms

dried black wood ear mushrooms

dried white cloud mushrooms

dried mixed forest mushrooms

dried shiitake mushrooms

dried kidney beans

dried black beans

dried cannellini beans

dried mung beans

dried chickpeas

yellow split peas

green split peas

barley

red lentils

du puy lentils

regular brown lentils

chana dahl

moong dahl

freekeh

burghul (bulgur wheat)

popcorn, always organic

sugar, always organic

raw sugar

brown sugar

caster (superfine) sugar

coconut sugar

whole raw almonds

raw cashews

almond meal

raw peanuts

raw pepitas (pumpkin seeds)

plain (all-purpose) flour

wholemeal (whole-wheat) flour

chickpea flour (besan)

vital wheat gluten flour

low gluten flour

cornflour (cornstarch)

tapioca flour

rice flour

desiccated (shredded) coconut

cocoa powder

agar

dried instant yeast

balsamic vinegar (a cheap one and an expensive one)

white vinegar

white wine vinegar

red wine vinegar

sherry vinegar (banderra roja is my favourite right now)

black vinegar

rice wine vinegar

apple cider vinegar

vegan fish sauce

soy sauce (dark and light)

kecap manis

Shao xing cooking wine

mirin

pomegranate molasses

mushroom oyster sauce

liquid smoke

Maggi seasoning

worcestershire sauce

vanilla essence

every kind of hot sauce

gochujang (Korean red pepper paste)

white miso paste

agave syrup

coconut nectar

maple syrup

corn tortillas

flour tortillas

pickled jalapeños

protein powder (lots)

oats

tricolour quinoa

cinnamon (ground and sticks)

fennel seeds

nutmeg, whole

Old Bay Seasoning

carraway seeds

roasted sesame seeds

Chinese five-spice

truffle salt

salt flakes

standard fine cooking salt or kosher salt

rock salt

smoked salt

black salt, colour

black salt, sulfuric

cardamom (pods and ground)

cumin seeds (ground and seeds)

paprika (smoked and sweet, Spanish only, no exception)

ground turmeric

mixed spice (sweet)

garlic powder

onion powder

black mustard seeds

allspice (savoury, pimento)

celery salt

chilli flakes

cayenne

mustard powder

curry powder

shichimi togarashi (Japanese chilli powder)

coriander (ground and seeds)

You know where to go in the event of a zombie apocalypse.

baking powder

baking soda
(bicarbonate of soda)

whole star anise

black sesame seeds

black peppercorns

cloves

Sichuan peppercorns

dried oregano

saffron threads

ground ginger

bay leaves (dried
and fresh)

frozen peas

frozen corn

frozen spinach

frozen broad (fava)
beans

frozen edamame

frozen dumplings

frozen blueberries

frozen mango
(I freeze it when
it's in season)

frozen grated ginger

frozen kaffir lime
leaves

frozen curry leaves

ice cream

sorbets (lemon,
passionfruit)

veggie beef
burger patties (for
emergency use)

flat-leaf parsley

coriander (cilantro)

thyme

mint

dill

basil

rosemary

celery

carrots

onions
(red and brown)

garlic

spring onions
(scallions)

mushrooms

capsicums (bell
peppers)

chillies

broccoli

spinach

bok choy

kale

some type of lettuce

avocados

potatoes (red skin
because they're an
all-rounder)

sweet potatoes

tomatoes

granny smiths (for
cooking)

pink ladies (for
eating)

oranges

lemons

limes

tinned chipotles in
adobo

tinned hearts of
palm

ajvar

curry ketchup

tomatillos

preserved lemons

dried ancho chilli

dried morita chilli

dried guajillo chilli

dried pastilla chilli

dried chipotle chilli

dried mulato chilli

jarred nopales

paella seasoning

tinned chestnuts

wholegrain bread

Vegemite

margarine

popcorn

salt

pepper

nutritional yeast

olive oil spray

tinned soup

2-minute noodles

veg bouillon

pasta

pasta sauce

cold-brew coffee

fizzy water

BBQ sauce

ALL the hot sauces

Sriracha

hot mustard

cayenne pepper

olive oil

tamari

peanut butter

**I won't allow but
wish to have:**

chips

tortilla chips

pretzels

anything packaged
and salty and
delicious

Go to Shannon's. It's better there.

SALADS

For the first time in her career, Shannon has made, embraced and fallen in love with salads. This chapter is probably one of the most stand-up salad sections of all time due to the flavours, substance, colours and, of course, how god-damn full you feel after eating them. We argue you can make friends with any of these salads and we have the customers to prove it.

WARM HEARTS OF PALM SALAD

This was a beautiful dish used to introduce hearts of palm to the S&D diner's palate. The layered and soft texture of the palm is unusual and tastes so good dusted with cornflour (cornstarch) and lightly fried. It was also a great way to showcase Shannon's impeccable guac and pico de gallo salsa.

Serves 4–6

425 g (15 oz) tinned hearts of palm, drained and rinsed (see note)

60 g (2 oz/½ cup) cornflour (cornstarch)

½ teaspoon ground cumin

½ teaspoon ground coriander

½ teaspoon chipotle powder (substitute cayenne powder, if unavailable)

¼ teaspoon salt

¼ teaspoon pepper

vegetable oil, for shallow-frying

1 quantity Fresh Guacamole (page 60)

Salsa

1 large green capsicum (bell pepper), seeds removed and cut into ½ cm (¼ in) dice

3 large tomatoes, seeds removed and cut into ½ cm (¼ in) dice

½ large onion, cut into ½ cm (¼ in) dice

1 large jalapeño, seeds removed and finely chopped

1 teaspoon crushed garlic

½ teaspoon salt flakes

¼ teaspoon cracked black pepper

1 tablespoon sherry vinegar

1 tablespoon extra-virgin olive oil

large handful coriander (cilantro), chopped, plus extra to serve (optional)

To make the salsa, mix all of the ingredients except the coriander in a large bowl and set aside for at least 30 minutes to allow the flavours to develop. Stir through the coriander just before serving.

Depending on the size of the palm hearts, either slice them in half on an angle or slice into thick discs on an angle.

Combine the cornflour, spices, salt and pepper in a bowl and toss through the palm hearts to coat evenly.

Pour the vegetable oil into a frying pan until 1 cm (½ in) deep and heat over high heat until hot but not smoking. Shake off the excess flour from the palm slices and gently place in the oil. Fry on all sides until golden brown and crisp. Alternatively, you can deep-fry the palm slices.

Make a thick line of guacamole down the centre of a serving platter, then place the salsa on top. Place the fried palm slices on the salsa so they are at different angles. Scatter with extra coriander (if using) and serve.

Note: Hearts of palm can be tricky to find if you don't have a Latin deli or specialty supermarket in your area. The closest substitute would be white asparagus – you can even be naughty and use tinned white asparagus, as it has a similar texture to hearts of palm, and you're frying it anyway. (Never again will we ever recommend using tinned asparagus.)

ARTICHOKE & CHICKPEA SALAD

This is still the longest-standing salad on our menu. And that says a lot for a chef who loves to change her menu twice each season. It just has to stay – customers love it far too much! For a summery variation, we like to swap chickpeas for chargrilled zucchinis (courgettes).

Preheat the oven to 180°C (350°F).

Toss the chickpeas in a little extra-virgin olive oil, smoked paprika and salt in a roasting tin. Roast in the oven for 20 minutes until crisp.

New-season Jerusalem artichokes don't need to be peeled as they have thin skins. Otherwise, peel the artichokes before cutting into bite-sized pieces. Place in an ovenproof dish and toss through some olive oil and the thyme. Season with salt and pepper. Add a splash of water and cover with foil. Roast for about 30 minutes, then remove the foil and roast for a further 15 minutes until lightly golden.

If using tinned or defrosted artichoke hearts, combine in a small bowl with a drizzle of extra-virgin olive oil and season with salt and pepper. Heat a chargrill pan to high and grill the artichokes, turning once, until chargrill marks appear. (If using pre-grilled and marinated artichokes, you can skip this step altogether.)

Combine the rocket, both types of artichokes, chickpeas and slivered almonds in a large bowl.

Sprinkle with salt and pepper and pour over your desired amount of salad dressing. Toss well to combine and transfer to a serving dish.

Heat about 1 cm (½ in) of vegetable oil in a small saucepan and gently drop the capers in. They will spit a little, so be careful. Fry for about 30 seconds until crisp, then drain on paper towel.

Sprinkle over the salad and serve immediately.

Serves 4–6

330 g (11½ oz) cooked or tinned chickpeas, drained and rinsed

extra-virgin olive oil

1 teaspoon smoked paprika

500 g (1 lb 2 oz) Jerusalem artichokes

1 tablespoon roughly chopped thyme

6 artichoke hearts, quartered (tinned or frozen are fine; or use marinated artichokes at a pinch)

2 large handfuls rocket (arugula)

small handful slivered almonds, toasted

Lemon & Cumin Vinaigrette (page 149)

vegetable oil, for frying

45 g (1½ oz/¼ cup) capers in vinegar, drained

109

PERUVIAN PURPLE POTATO & PUMPKIN SALAD

This dish was an answer to customers saying they wanted healthier, fresher options. There's some health in here ... It's colourful and beautiful, the dressing is sensational, but at the end of the day ... potatoes.

Serves 4–6

600 g (1 lb 5 oz) (about 10) purple congo potatoes

1 kg (2 lb 3 oz) Japanese pumpkin (kabocha squash) or any firm pumpkin, peeled, seeds removed and cut into 3–4 cm (1¼–1½ in) cubes

70 g (2½ oz/½ cup) pepitas (pumpkin seeds), toasted

large handful flat-leaf parsley leaves

large handful coriander (cilantro) leaves

small handful Pickled Onions (page 136)

Smoked Paprika Vinaigrette (page 149)

Place the potatoes in a large saucepan, cover with cold water and bring to the boil. Reduce the heat to a simmer and cook for 20–30 minutes, until the potatoes can be easily pierced with a knife. Drain and peel when cool enough to handle. (This may be a little easier said than done; sometimes you can slip skins off with your hands, sometimes you'll need a peeler, and sometimes the side of a spoon.)

Meanwhile, steam the pumpkin in a steamer for 15–20 minutes until just tender – do not overcook.

Transfer the potato and pumpkin to a salad bowl and set aside in the fridge to cool completely.

Add the pepitas, herbs and pickled onions to the salad and pour over enough dressing to coat. Toss thoroughly to combine and serve.

Note: Shannon once dated a guy who didn't like potatoes. Needless to say it didn't work out.

110

SPANISH CHARGRILLED CAPSICUM SALAD

Don't be fooled by the name or the simplicity of this dish. It sounds really '90s, we get it. We both lived through the sundried tomato and capsicum (bell pepper) craze. This is not that. It's still what Shannon eats with her dad. She grew up eating this dish. It's fresh, and perfect served on toasted bread.

Heat a chargrill pan over high heat, add the whole capsicums and cook until blackened (you may need to do this in batches, depending on the size of your pan). Transfer to a zip lock bag or place in a bowl and cover with plastic wrap. Set aside to steam for about 10 minutes.

Remove the skins from the capsicums and slice the flesh into 1 cm (½ in) thick strips. Transfer to a bowl and add the remaining ingredients, tossing well to combine. Set aside in the fridge for at least 1 hour, but it will taste even better if left until the next day.

Serves 4–6

3 large green capsicums (bell peppers)

3 large red capsicums (bell peppers)

2 shallots, very finely chopped

1 large garlic clove, crushed

½ teaspoon dried oregano

small handful flat-leaf parsley, finely chopped

1½ teaspoon salt flakes

½ teaspoon ground black pepper

2½ tablespoons sherry vinegar (substitute red wine vinegar if you can't find it)

80 ml (2½ fl oz/⅓ cup) extra-virgin olive oil

115

BRAZILIAN SLAW

As far as salads go, you just don't get prettier, with more texture, more variety and more fun.

Serves 4–6

1½ tablespoons olive oil

150 g (5½ oz) fresh or frozen corn kernels

85 g (3 oz) oyster mushrooms, roughly torn

1 tablespoon tamari or soy sauce

1 granny smith apple, cored and cut into thin matchsticks

1 large carrot, peeled and cut into thin matchsticks

½ red onion, thinly sliced

85 g (3 oz) green pimento olives, sliced into thin rounds

300 g (10½ oz) thinly shredded purple cabbage

large handful flat-leaf parsley leaves

large handful coriander (cilantro) leaves

Dressing

250 g (9 oz/1 cup) Aioli (page 152)

zest and juice of 1 lime

1 small garlic clove, crushed

Garnish

3 corn tortillas, cut into 5 mm (¼ in) strips (or use roughly crushed tortilla chips)

olive oil spray

chilli and lime salt (see note)

Preheat the oven to 180°C (350°F).

Heat 2 teaspoons of the oil in a chargrill pan or small frying pan. Grill or sauté the corn until lightly charred. Remove from the heat and set aside.

Heat the remaining oil in a medium-sized frying pan over medium heat. Add the mushrooms and soy sauce and sauté until golden and slightly crisp. Set aside to cool.

To make the dressing, combine the ingredients in a bowl and whisk together until well combined.

To build the salad, combine all of the ingredients in a large salad bowl and add enough of the dressing to lightly coat. Season with salt and pepper, to taste.

For the garnish, spray the tortilla strips with olive oil spray and dust with a little chilli and lime salt. Transfer to a baking tray and bake in the oven until crisp. If you are using tortilla chips, just sprinkle with the chilli and lime salt instead.

Build a small conical tower with the salad and top with the garnish. Big salads are always better, especially when tortilla chips are involved.

Note: Chilli and lime salt can be found at any Latin supermarket, or you can simply use salt instead.

ARCO IRIS SALAD

Seasonal Tomato & Quinoa Salad

Like most salads, this one is contingent on being super fresh. Make sure you use the most beautiful fresh tomatoes, avocado and asparagus possible. We love this salad, especially because when plated it's just this side of too beautiful to eat.

Place the rinsed quinoa in a small saucepan with a pinch of salt and 185 ml (6½ fl oz/¾ cup) cold water. Bring to the boil uncovered then, once boiling, cover and reduce the heat to a low simmer. Cook for 8–10 minutes, until the liquid has been absorbed and the quinoa is cooked through.

Drizzle the asparagus with olive oil and sprinkle with a little salt and pepper. Heat a chargrill pan over high heat and grill the spears until dark char marks appear all over.

Transfer the asparagus to a bowl and add the tomatoes, avocado and pickled onion. Drizzle over enough basil dressing to lightly coat and toss to combine.

Arrange a few lettuce leaves in a serving bowl and top with the salad to the side. Scatter over a few basil leaves and serve.

Serves 4–6

100 g (3½ oz/½ cup) tricolour quinoa, rinsed (or any quinoa you have available)

1 bunch (about 12 spears) asparagus, woody ends snapped off

olive oil, for drizzling

2 large black tomatoes, cut into wedges

10 red cherry tomatoes, halved

10 yellow cherry tomatoes, halved

1 avocado, diced

small handful Pickled Onions (page 136)

Smashed Basil Dressing (page 149)

handful cos (romaine) lettuce leaves, to serve

small handful basil leaves, to serve

ENSALADA CRUJIENTE

Pickled Radish & Cucumber Salad

Hands down, top summer salad. Give us nothing but this if the temperature reaches beach weather. Please. Thank you.

Serves 4–6

2 baby cos (romaine) lettuce, leaves separated and rinsed

1 radicchio, leaves separated and rinsed

1 Lebanese (short) cucumber, sliced

2 large handfuls Pickled Radishes (page 136)

small handful Pickled Onions (page 136)

1 avocado, roughly diced

Creamy Lime & Coriander Dressing (page 150)

small handful dill, chopped

Place the lettuce and radicchio leaves in a large serving dish, then scatter over the cucumber, pickled radish and onion, and avocado.

Drizzle with enough of the dressing to lightly coat the salad, then sprinkle over the dill. Season to taste, and serve.

ENSALADA CON PATATAS BRAVAS

Spanish Potato Salad

We know … Patatas bravas is normally a fried potato dish. This is a spin on the heavy, fried, unhealthy classic version. This recipe is fresher and brighter, and one that is still awesome. But, honestly, we love it both ways. Go ahead, fry or bake the potatoes and toss the sauce through. But seriously, who doesn't love potato salad? And no eggs means you can take this to picnics and have a light, tangy, spicy alternative that won't go toxic in the sun.

If you want to peel the potatoes, do it – be a weirdo. But why bother? Weirdo.

Otherwise, place the potatoes in a large saucepan and cover with cold water. Add the salt and bring to the boil. Reduce the heat to a simmer and cook until the potatoes can be just pierced through with a knife. Drain and transfer to a large bowl.

To make the Bravas dressing, blend all of the ingredients except the olive oil in a blender. With motor running, slowly add the oil. Season with salt and pepper, to taste.

Add the remaining salad ingredients to the potatoes and pour over enough dressing to coat really well. The potatoes will soak up quite a lot of the dressing, so add a little more than you think it needs. Check and adjust the seasoning, if necessary.

Serves 4–6

1 kg (2 lb 3 oz) kipfler potatoes

1 tablespoon salt

½ red onion, thinly sliced into strips

2 large tomatoes, seeds removed and sliced into thin strips

330 g (11½ oz) cooked or tinned chickpeas, drained and rinsed

small handful flat-leaf parsley, roughly chopped

Bravas Dressing

4 tablespoons ajvar (red capsicum/pepper relish)

2 tablespoons sherry vinegar

½ tomato, seeds removed

1 large garlic clove

1 teaspoon chilli flakes

¼ teaspoon ground cumin

½ teaspoon ground turmeric

½ teaspoon oregano

1 teaspoon smoked paprika

125 ml (4 fl oz/½ cup) extra-virgin olive oil

123

MELON SALAD WITH PICKLED PINEAPPLE & JALAPEÑO

This dish is another misunderstood menu item. We should start an anonymous group for misunderstood dishes. Especially because when customers love a misunderstood dish, they become nearly obsessed with it. But those with a specialised palate like this are few and far between. Often, you'll find me and Shannon eating this with our fingers in the kitchen at the end of service singing 'your loss' and 'more for me'.

While to the naked eye this might be considered a fruit salad, it's far from it. This dish is meant to be a bright, spicy and fresh addition to your meal and when prepared properly – with melon, pickled pineapple and jalapeño to make the perfect bite – it is simply stunning.

Serves 4–6

½ pineapple, peeled, core removed and flesh sliced lengthways into long thin strips

2 jalapeños, very thinly sliced

½ honeydew melon, peeled, seeds removed and flesh thinly sliced

¼ watermelon, cut into small triangles

½ rockmelon (cantaloupe), cut into cubes

sea salt flakes

handful mint leaves

Pickle Brine

250 ml (8½ fl oz/1 cup) apple cider vinegar

230 g (8 oz/1 cup) caster (superfine) sugar

juice and zest of 1 orange

juice and zest of 1 lime

½ teaspoon cumin seeds

2 whole cloves

1 garlic clove, smashed

1 cinnamon stick, broken in half

small handful coriander (cilantro) stems (only if you have them on hand)

1 fresh bay leaf

½ teaspoon whole peppercorns

To make the pickle brine, place all of the ingredients in a medium-sized saucepan and bring to the boil over high heat. Reduce the heat to a simmer and cook until the sugar is completely dissolved. Remove from the heat and set aside for 15 minutes to allow the flavours to infuse.

Place the pineapple and jalapeño in a large bowl and pour over the pickle brine, bits and all.

Pickle the pineapple and jalapeño for at least 3 hours before using, but the longer this sits the better it gets, so if you can, try to give it at least 24 hours.

To build the salad, lay the honeydew slices on a large serving plate and loosely arrange the watermelon and rockmelon over the top – don't make it look too perfect if you can help it. Lay the pickled pineapple and jalapeño over and in between the melon pieces.

Use a spoon to drizzle the pickle brine over the salad – this will act as your dressing. Scatter with the smallest amount of salt flakes, a crack of black pepper and a handful of picked mint leaves.

ENSALADA DE FLORES DE BRÓCOLI Y COLIFLOR

Chargrilled Broccoli & Cauliflower Salad

Like many dishes that Shannon invents, she refers to them as flukes, but really we all know they're beautiful, calculated and methodical. She knows what she's doing. This salad came about as a weather change necessity; it originated as a deep-fried broccoli and cauliflower fritter dish that included the Salsa Verde as a drizzle and pepitas. Needless to say, it did really well for us, 'cause, yum. But the salad exceeded its deep-fried counterpart. However, if you do want that deep-fried sensation, please feel free to get ambitious and batter up.

Bring a large saucepan of salted water to the boil, then add the broccoli, cauliflower and cabbage. Blanch the vegetables for 1–2 minutes until they are just beginning to soften.

Heat a chargrill pan over high heat.

Drain the vegetables and transfer to a large bowl. Drizzle over a little olive oil and season with salt and pepper.

Add the vegetables to the chargrill pan and cook, in batches if necessary, on both sides until chargrill lines appear. Return to the bowl. Add the remaining ingredients, keeping back a small handful of pepitas.

Smear the salsa verde dressing on a serving platter and top with the salad. Scatter over the remaining pepitas and serve.

Serves 4–6

2 broccoli heads, cut into large florets

½ cauliflower, cut into large florets

½ small purple cabbage, leaves roughly torn into large pieces

olive oil, for drizzling

large handful flat-leaf parsley leaves

large handful coriander (cilantro) leaves

70 g (2½ oz/½ cup) pepitas (pumpkin seeds), toasted

small handful Pickled Onions (page 136)

Salsa Verde (page 155)

Pimento
RAISINS
cumin seeds
Ginger
Yeast
Cin Stix
PEPPER
CLOVES
ancho powder for ganache
Pepitas
Pimento
FENNEL SEEDS

EXTRAS

This chapter is for all the extra bits that didn't fit into other categories, but things you won't want to pass up – pickled veg, cashew cheese … see, told you so. Shannon has many tricks up her culinary sleeves and these little additions are guaranteed to make any meal just that little bit better.

MEXICAN RED RICE

Red, red riiiiice, stay close to meeeeee. Don't let me be alone. Red, red rice you make me feel so fine.

Red rice is like plain rice, but way, way, waaaaayyyy better. Go to the effort, make yourself red rice with all your Latin dishes.

Serves 4–6

2 tablespoons olive oil

1 jalapeño, finely diced

2 garlic cloves, crushed

1 small white onion, finely chopped

1 teaspoon cumin seeds

400 g (14 oz/2 cups) long-grain
white rice

125 g (4½ oz) tinned diced tomatoes

1 litre (34 fl oz/4 cups) chicken
or vegetable stock

1 fresh bay leaf

1 teaspoon dried oregano

155 g (5½ oz/1 cup) frozen peas, thawed

handful coriander (cilantro), roughly
chopped

Heat the olive oil in a medium-sized saucepan over medium heat. Add the jalapeño, garlic, onion and cumin seeds and cook, stirring frequently, until soft.

Add the rice and cook for a few minutes until it just begins to take on some colour. Stir in the tomatoes and cook for a few minutes, then add the stock, bay leaf and oregano. Increase the heat to high and bring the rice to the boil, then reduce the heat to as low as it can go and cook the rice for about 20 minutes, until all of the stock has been absorbed.

Remove the rice from the heat and add the peas and coriander. Season with salt and pepper, then fluff with a fork and allow to steam off the heat for a few minutes before serving.

BRAISED BARLEY & PEAS

This side dish was the carrier for our Spanish Meatballs (page 89) on our Smith & Daughters winter 2014 menu. It's super hearty and filling, perfect for hibernation season.

Pour the stock into a large saucepan and bring to the boil. Reduce the heat to low and keep warm while you make the barley.

Heat the oil and 2 tablespoons of the butter in a large saucepan over low heat. Add the onion, thyme and rosemary, and a pinch of salt and pepper. Cook for about 5 minutes or until the onion is beginning to turn golden, then add the crushed garlic and cook for a further 1 minute.

Pour the barley into the pan and stir well. Cook for 1 minute to slightly toast the grains.

Add one-quarter of the stock to the pan, one ladleful at a time, and cook the barley, stirring frequently. Once the stock is absorbed, add another quarter of the stock and continue cooking and stirring until all the stock has been used. The barley should be nice and creamy but still a little wet.

Remove from the heat and stir through the remaining butter, lemon zest, peas and parsley.

Check the seasoning and adjust to taste, if necessary.

Serves 4–6

2 litres (68 fl oz/8 cups) chicken or vegetable stock

1 tablespoon olive oil

3 tablespoons butter

1 onion, chopped

1 teaspoon chopped thyme

1 teaspoon chopped rosemary

2 large garlic cloves, crushed

440 g (15½ oz/2 cups) pearled barley

zest of ½ lemon

80 g (2¾ oz/½ cup) frozen peas, thawed

handful fresh flat-leaf parsley, roughly chopped

135

PICKLED ONIONS (& OTHER STUFF)

Use this pickle solution to pickle anything – all your favourite stuff. At the restaurant we use finely shredded pickled cabbage as well as these onions on quite a lot of dishes. Become familiar with this recipe and you'll be friends with a lot of other recipes in our book. And friends with us, because we LOVE pickled stuff!

Serves 4–6

2 large red onions, halved and thinly sliced

boiling water

220 g (8 oz/1 cup) sugar

250 ml (8½ fl oz/1 cup) apple cider vinegar

juice of 3 limes

1 teaspoon cumin seeds

1 cinnamon stick

3 whole cloves

2 strips of orange peel

5 peppercorns

½ teaspoon dried oregano

½ teaspoon chilli flakes

1 teaspoon salt

Place the onion in a heatproof bowl and pour over enough boiling water to cover. Stand for 30 seconds (you're not cooking the onion, but taking the harshness out of them), then drain and set aside in a bowl.

Place the remaining ingredients in a small saucepan and bring to the boil. Reduce the heat to a low simmer and cook until the sugar is dissolved.

Pour the pickling solution over the onion and set aside to infuse for at least 2 hours before eating. The pickled onion will keep for up to 2 weeks in the fridge.

Note: To pickle other veg, chop them how you like, then follow the above steps except the boiling.

GARLIC & CHILLI KALE

We use this kale in our Brekkie Burritos (page 32), but it's super yum and full of health, so eat it as a side dish to anything in this book. It came to our attention that there's a zillion recipes for kale (ever since the Kale Craze of '06) and we just thought we'd throw in our two cents. This is our favourite way, but if you have your own favourite way to prepare kale, use that instead. Who cares, as long as you're not over-cooking it and it still tastes good ... Don't screw up the kale.

Bring a large saucepan of salted water to the boil. Drop in the kale or cavolo nero leaves and blanch for about 2 minutes or until slightly softened (do not overcook). Drain and refresh under cold water.

Heat the oil in a large frying pan over medium heat. Add the garlic and chilli flakes and cook, stirring frequently, until the garlic is just starting to colour. Add the kale and stir well to coat in all the yummy garlic and chilli oil. Increase the heat to high and cook for 1 minute, then finish with a squeeze of lemon juice and salt and pepper, to taste.

Serves 4–6

1 bunch kale or cavolo nero, leaves stripped and roughly chopped into large pieces

2 tablespoons extra-virgin olive oil

2 large garlic cloves, thinly sliced

½ teaspoon chilli flakes

juice of ½ lemon

CHIPOTLE CASHEW CHEESE

At the restaurant, this firm cheese is added to our Brekkie Burritos (page 32) for an extra bit of zing, but really this can and should be eaten with anything. Like its non-vegan counterpart, cheese is king.

Serves 4–6

235 g (8½ oz/1½ cups) raw cashews, soaked for at least 2 hours in cold water

60 ml (2 fl oz/¼ cup) apple cider vinegar

2 tablespoons lime juice

3 tablespoons nutritional yeast

1 teaspoon salt

½ teaspoon ground cumin

2 chipotles in adobo

Blend all of the ingredients in a blender along with 2 tablespoons water. You may have to stop the blender every 10 seconds or so and give the mix a bit of a stir to help move it around. Add extra water, 1 tablespoon at a time, and blend for at least 2 minutes or until the mixture is completely smooth or to your desired consistency (see note).

Transfer to a bowl and refrigerate until the cheese has firmed up and chilled completely.

Note: For a more spreadable, cream cheese-like texture, add up to 6 tablespoons water. For a firmer cheese, use as little extra water as possible.

A: ROXY MUSIC *Latin SPANISH Anything CUBAN JAZZ

B: SLAYER CRADLE OF FILTH NIN Marilyn Manson

C: Nina Simone AC/DC SIMPLY RED Sade eURYTHMICs Etta James FLEETWOOD MAC

D: the doors SISTER ACT 2: CREEDENCE CLEARWATER REVIVAL TALKING HEADS 90s HIP HOP MORRISSEY THE SMITHS THE CURE Siouxsie and the Banshees NewOrder DIE ANTWOORD DEPECHE MODE

E: COMBICHRIST

F: DRAKE Celine DION U2 indie rock Taylor Swift Katy Perry

A: Favourite is mostly Latin – to get into the vibe.

B: If it's 30 minutes until service and there's still heaps to do. (These artists can also be effectively used to teach a hungover dishie a lesson.)

C: Music I like that reminds me of my mum when I cook.

D: If we're on point for service, ready to go and having fun. | E: The one band I put on to let the staff know I'm not impressed.

F: Music not allowed in my kitchen.

SAUCES & DRESSINGS

A saucy section created for you by a saucy gal – both in temperament and preference. Shannon loves a good drenching of dressing and coating of sauce. That's where the extra flavours come from! We recommend you make heaps of these and play around with them. We never tie any dressings to one salad. Shannon's dressings are light, bright, bold and delicious. Use the freshest ingredients you can find – the fresher the herbs and citrus, the better the dressing. Also, we definitely recommend all of the sauces to go with a big bowl of hot, salty chips. Make them all. You won't regret it.

GREEN APPLE &
JALAPEÑO HOT SAUCE

GREEN APPLE & JALAPEÑO HOT SAUCE

This hot sauce is how we got the media to come to the opening of the restaurant. Part of our media kits included tiny branded Smith & Daughters bottles of it. We even got emails later saying how they wanted to buy it, that they would come just for the sauce, and that they were eating it drop by drop to make it last longer.

We encourage you to put this on everything; it's literally our most favourite hot sauce that we've ever made. WE LOVE THIS SAUCE.

1 kg (2 lb 3 oz) jalapeños, 500 g (1 lb 2 oz) left whole; 500 g (1 lb 2 oz) seeds removed

80 ml (2½ fl oz/⅓ cup) olive oil

1 large onion, chopped

5 garlic cloves, crushed

1 teaspoon ground cumin

1 teaspoon salt

500 ml (17 fl oz/2 cups) apple cider vinegar

500 ml (17 fl oz/2 cups) freshly squeezed granny smith apple juice (either do this yourself or buy as fresh as possible – your local juice shop should be able to do it for you)

juice of 2 limes

330 g (11½ oz/1½ cups) sugar

80 g (2¾ oz/⅓ cup) brown sugar

½ bunch coriander (cilantro)

Process the jalapeños in a food processor or blender until finely chopped.

Heat the oil in a large saucepan over medium heat. Add the onion, garlic, cumin and salt and cook, stirring occasionally, until soft. Add the puréed chillies and cook for a further 5 minutes.

Add the vinegar, apple juice, lime juice, sugars and 500 ml (17 fl oz/2 cups) cold water, and stir to combine. Reduce the heat to low and simmer for 1 hour.

Remove from the heat and set aside to cool to room temperature. Transfer the mixture to a food processor or blender, add the coriander and blend until very smooth.

Pour into containers or jars and store in the fridge for up to 1 month.

CHIMICHURRI

This is a traditional Argentinian sauce, typically served with grilled meats, so it pairs awesomely with vegan steaks or chicken fillets, tofu, etc. A very good all-rounder, we use it as a salad dressing, dipping sauce, and often stir it through Garlic Aioli (page 152) for a creamy variation. Because really, aioli makes everything taste better.

zest of ½ orange plus 1 tablespoon juice

large handful coriander (cilantro), chopped

large handful flat-leaf parsley, chopped

2 spring onions (scallions), chopped

1 tablespoon sherry vinegar

1 small red chilli, (seeds removed for a milder sauce)

1 tablespoon capers

½ teaspoon cumin seeds

60 ml (2 fl oz/¼ cup) vegetable oil

60 ml (2 fl oz/¼ cup) extra-virgin olive oil

Place all of the ingredients except the oils in a blender or food processor and blend until finely chopped.

With the motor running, slowly pour in the oils until well combined. Season to taste.

SMASHED BASIL DRESSING

30 g (1 oz) basil leaves

juice of 1 medium-sized lemon

1 teaspoon sugar

1 tablespoon dijon mustard

1 teaspoon salt

½ teaspoon black pepper

80 ml (2½ fl oz/⅓ cup) olive oil

Place all of the ingredients except the olive oil in a blender or jug.

With the motor set to low or whisking by hand, slowly drizzle in the oil until well combined and emulsified. If you prefer a slightly thinner dressing, drizzle in a little hot water after the oil.

LEMON & CUMIN VINAIGRETTE

60 ml (2 fl oz/¼ cup) lemon juice

1 teaspoon cumin seeds

1 tablespoon agave syrup

½ tablespoon dijon mustard

½ teaspoon salt

½ teaspoon pepper

80 ml (2½ fl oz/⅓ cup) extra-virgin olive oil

Place the lemon juice, cumin seeds, agave syrup, mustard, salt and pepper in a blender or jug.

With the motor set to low or whisking by hand, slowly drizzle in the oil until well combined and emulsified.

SMOKED PAPRIKA VINAIGRETTE

60 ml (2 fl oz/¼ cup) sherry vinegar

1 small thyme sprig, leaves picked and chopped

1 teaspoon salt

½ teaspoon black pepper

1 tablespoon dijon mustard

1 teaspoon agave syrup

½ teaspoon cumin seeds

1 teaspoon smoked paprika

pinch of dried oregano

½ small garlic clove, finely chopped

125 ml (4 fl oz/½ cup) extra-virgin olive oil

Place all of the ingredients except the olive oil in a blender or jug.

With the motor set to low or whisking by hand, slowly drizzle in the oil until well combined and emulsified.

CREAMY LIME & CORIANDER DRESSING

250 g (9 oz/1 cup) Garlic Aioli
(page 152)

zest of ½ lime

juice of 1 lime

1 teaspoon agave syrup

small handful coriander (cilantro),
chopped

Place all of the ingredients in a jug or blender and whisk or
blend until bright green.

Add a little water at the end if you prefer a thinner dressing.

CORIANDER PESTO

At the restaurant and deli, we make our pestos with roasted pepitas (pumpkin seeds) or sunflower seeds so they're safe for our nut allergy customers. If you want to use nuts (pine nuts/cashews etc.), go ahead.

1 bunch coriander (cilantro)

small handful flat-leaf parsley

small handful mint

1 green jalapeño

2 garlic cloves, peeled

30 g (1 oz/¼ cup) pepitas (pumpkin seeds), toasted

juice of 1 lime

45 g (1½ oz/¼ cup) capers

125 ml (4 fl oz/½ cup) vegetable oil

Place all of the ingredients except the oil in a food processor or blender and process on high speed until mashed up. Add a little drizzle of the oil to help get the mixture moving, if necessary.

With the motor running, slowly drizzle in the oil until incorporated and emulsified.

CORIANDER CASHEW CREAM

Use this cream anywhere you would use sour cream in a recipe.

155 g (5½ oz/1 cup) raw cashews, soaked (we use broken cashew pieces which only have to be soaked for 1 hour, but if you can only find whole cashews, soak them for at least 5 hours)

juice of 1 lemon

1 tablespoon apple cider vinegar

large handful coriander (cilantro), stalks and leaves roughly chopped

1 teaspoon salt

Rinse and drain the cashews, then place in a blender with the remaining ingredients and 170 ml (5½ fl oz/⅔ cup) cold water.

Blend on medium speed for a few minutes until smooth. Add a little more water if you prefer a slightly thinner cream.

AVOCADO CREAM

It's like when two of your favourite things come together to become even better. Avocado + Aioli forever.

1 large avocado

juice of 1 lime

80 g (2¾ oz/⅓ cup) Garlic Aioli (page 152)

1 tablespoon roughly chopped coriander (cilantro) leaves

1 teaspoon salt

Place all of the ingredients in a blender and blend until smooth.

It's best to eat this on the day you make it, but it will keep in an airtight container with plastic wrap covering the surface of the cream for up to 2 days in the fridge.

GARLIC AIOLI

Our aioli is one of the main Smith & Daughters customer freak-out menu items. It is also one of Shannon's holy grails as far as recipes go. While there are heaps of vegan aiolis out there now, this one took Shannon 10 years to perfect, and to this day forms the base of so much goodness in our restaurant and deli. So creamy and garlicky, and free of eggs, it's ace for pregnant people, and those with allergies and intolerances. This recipe doubles very well.

115 g (4 oz) silken tofu

1 teaspoon crushed garlic

1 teaspoon salt

60 ml (2 fl oz/¼ cup) soy milk

2 teaspoons apple cider vinegar

2 teaspoons dijon mustard

125 ml (4 fl oz/½ cup) vegetable oil

125 ml (4 fl oz/½ cup) extra-virgin olive oil

Place all of the ingredients except the oils in a blender and blend until well combined.

With the motor running on medium speed, slowly drizzle in the oils until well combined and emulsified.

CHIPOTLE AIOLI

Spice it up, add some pizzazz. The best thing about chipotles is their amazing ability to add a rich smokiness to everything. So when adding to aioli, you've already pretty much stepped up your spread/dip game to the highest level possible.

250 g (9 oz/1 cup) Garlic Aioli (see above)

chipotles in adobo, to taste

It's hard to say how many chipotles to add because it's all about preference. Place the aioli in a blender and add 1 chipotle. Blend, then taste to see if it needs another. Or add another 5 if that's what you want. It's up to you.

Blend until entirely smooth and incorporated. You may also want to have a big batch of wedges in the oven ready to go. Or hot chips … No judgement.

GARLIC AIOLI

SALSA VERDE

Salsa is the Mexican answer to making everything taste even better than it already does. Shannon has dreamt up three of her most favourite fresh salsa recipes that include texture, complexity and a delightful amount of bright flavours. Keep these around for chips and well, dumping on everything.

2 ancho chillies

60 g (2 oz/½ cup) raisins

1 jalapeño

5 garlic cloves, unpeeled

½ red onion

juice and zest of 1 lime

1 tablespoon dijon mustard

1 tablespoon sherry vinegar

2 tablespoons capers

2 large handfuls flat-leaf parsley, roughly chopped

large handful mint, roughly chopped

2 large handfuls coriander (cilantro), roughly chopped

large handful basil, roughly chopped

small handful oregano, roughly chopped

½ teaspoon cocoa powder

1 teaspoon ground cumin

1 tablespoon agave syrup, or whatever sweetener you like

125 ml (4 fl oz/½ cup) olive oil

Place the ancho chillies and raisins in a medium-sized saucepan and cover with water. Bring to the boil, then remove from the heat and set aside to soften in the water for 30 minutes. Drain.

Meanwhile, heat a chargrill pan over high heat and cook the jalapeño, garlic and red onion until blackened all over.

Peel the garlic, then transfer to a food processor along with the jalapeño and red onion. Add the drained ancho chillies and raisins along with the remaining ingredients except the oil, and blend thoroughly.

With the motor running, slowly add the oil until well combined. Season, to taste.

The salsa will keep for up to 4 days in the fridge.

FIRE-ROASTED TOMATO & CHIPOTLE SALSA

5 tomatoes (about 600 g/1 lb 5 oz)

1 red onion, halved

2 garlic cloves, peeled

2 chipotles in adobo

2 tablespoons adobo sauce

large handful coriander (cilantro), roughly chopped

juice of 1 lime

Heat a chargrill pan or barbecue over high heat and grill the tomatoes and onion until lightly blackened all over.

Transfer to a food processor along with the remaining ingredients. Season with salt and pepper and pulse until you have a slightly chunky salsa.

MANGO SALSA

2 firm ripe mangoes, diced

½ red capsicum (bell pepper), finely diced

½–1 green jalapeño, finely diced

½ red onion, finely chopped

small handful coriander (cilantro), roughly chopped

small handful mint, roughly chopped

juice of 1 lime

2 tablespoons hot sauce of your choice

2 tablespoons olive oil

Combine all of the ingredients in a bowl and season with salt and pepper. Set aside for at least 1 hour for the flavours to infuse.

SMOKY ROMESCO

This is a really classic, everyday Spanish sauce that Shannon grew up eating. Romesco is made using nuts. We've chosen almonds for this recipe but, by all means, use any nuts you have on hand. This recipe is also a great way to use up stale bread. There's really no limit to this sauce: pair it with green beans, zucchini (courgettes), pasta, potato salad, on bread. At the restaurant we combo it with Chargrilled Asparagus (page 69). But we've also slathered smashed fried baby potatoes with this and Chimichurri (page 148). We highly recommend you do this.

Makes about 500 g (1 lb 2 oz/2 cups)

2 large tomatoes

1 red capsicum (bell pepper)

145 ml (5 fl oz) olive oil

50 g (1¾ oz) bread (use gluten-free, if desired)

40 g (1¼ oz/¼ cup) almonds, toasted (replace with pepitas/pumpkin seeds or sunflower seeds for a nut-free version)

½ teaspoon chilli flakes

2 garlic cloves, peeled

small handful mint leaves, chopped

small handful flat-leaf parsley leaves, chopped

1 teaspoon ground cumin

2 teaspoons smoked paprika

60 ml (2 fl oz/¼ cup) Pedro Xímenez sherry (optional, but worth it)

juice of ½ lemon

1 tablespoon sherry vinegar

1 tablespoon capers

1 teaspoon salt flakes

½ teaspoon black pepper

Heat a chargrill pan over high heat and grill the tomatoes and capsicum until blackened all over. Alternatively, grill the veg under the grill (broiler) on a high heat. Transfer to a bowl and cover with plastic wrap for a few minutes to steam. When cool enough to handle, remove the skins. Do not rinse under water – a little bit of char is good.

Heat 1 tablespoon of the oil in a small frying pan over medium heat. Add the bread and fry until golden on both sides.

Transfer the bread to a food processor or blender and add all of the remaining ingredients except the remaining oil. Blend until smooth then, with the motor running, slowly add the oil until well combined. Check the seasoning and adjust to taste.

Romesco sauce will keep for up to 4 days in the fridge.

SOFRITO

Sofrito is the key to unlocking everything Spanish. Beyond Spanish cuisine, there are a million other uses for sofrito. It can be served with pasta if you're feeling lazy. Or for a jazzier lazy pasta, add olives, basil and capers. Or add soaked TVP and make it into a bolognese, or vegan tuna or chilli. It also makes a yum pizza sauce, or you can use it as a dipping sauce for bread. It's just that good. Sofrito is a great example of the difference between restaurant quality food and not. This recipe adds a richness and depth of flavour you don't typically find in home-cooked meals. To gain that richness and complexity is reason enough to go the extra mile and put the effort into making this sauce at home. It is easy to make but time-consuming. Make it on a Sunday, hanging out at the house, when you have time for something to sit on the stove. It's worth it.

Heat the oil in a saucepan over medium heat, then add the capsicum and onion. Reduce the temperature to low, add the salt and cook, stirring occasionally, for about 10 minutes or until the veg are very soft. Add the garlic and cook for a few minutes before adding the oregano, paprika and saffron. Cook for about 30 seconds, then add the tomato.

Cover the pan with a lid slightly ajar and cook on the lowest heat for 1 hour, until the sauce is very thick and rich.

Add the pepper and parsley and stir through. Check the seasoning and add more if you wish. If the tomatoes are a little too tart, add a pinch of sugar to balance the flavours.

Set aside to cool completely, then store in an airtight container covered with olive oil in the fridge. It will keep for at least 1 week.

If you want to make a double or triple batch, put it in small containers and freeze – it's good to have on hand for anything and everything.

Makes about 1 kg (2 lb 3 oz/4 cups)

80 ml (2½ fl oz/⅓ cup) olive oil, plus extra to cover

½ green capsicum (bell pepper), diced

½ red capsicum (bell pepper), diced

1 small onion, chopped

1 teaspoon salt

1 tablespoon crushed garlic

½ teaspoon fresh oregano

1 teaspoon sweet paprika

tiny pinch of saffron (don't worry if you don't have it)

800 g (1 lb 12 oz) tinned diced tomatoes

½ teaspoon black pepper

small handful flat-leaf parsley, chopped

pinch of sugar, if needed

159

SHANNON'S INSPIRATIONS

My mum – my mother is number one. She is so tough. She's come from nothing. She was an amazing fashion designer in the late 80s in Melbourne. A single parent who busted her arse. She sold her jewellery to send me to school and took three jobs to make sure that I could learn to cook. She has been through so much, cancer and all ... You know when you're a teenager and you're a little shit? I totally didn't appreciate it and that is my only regret in life – having been that arsehole. So now anything I can do for her I do. There is no way I could ever pay her back.

My grandma – especially for the foundation of Smith & Daughters and this book. She taught me about my Spanish heritage and showed me a world that was non-existent in Australia through all this incredible Spanish food. She gave me pride in who I am through something that is my greatest passion.

Travel – everywhere and anywhere.

Work inspirations – people thinking I can't do something.

MO'S INSPIRATIONS

My husband, Callum Preston – there's nothing he can't do, or won't learn how to do. He's made the life of a positive go-getter even more worthwhile and awesome. He's the greatest.

My parents – for working hard, teaching me the value of hard work, and making sure all opportunities were available to me and my siblings.

My grams, Dotty J – for being the most badass of all bad asses who ever lived. And for always, always having something to look forward to, and an occasion to wear something fancy.

My best friends Matt & Danielle Miller – pursuing goals and always setting the bar high in terms of being good friends, parents and professionals. Being with them is my island paradise.

People who know how to do lots of things and have lived a lot of lives.

PMA – positive mental attitude.

Leslie Knope – because positive is ALWAYS better than negative.

SWEET

Shannon's not a dessert girl, never has been, ever. The desserts in this chapter are designed to be light enough to enjoy even after you've eaten a big meal. To Shannon, cake is gross but doughnuts are awesome, they're the mid-point between savoury and sweet. And guess what? This section includes Shannon's famous warm Spanish doughnuts!

SPICED MEXICAN FLAN

This is not a super well-known dish in Australia. So often when we served it at the restaurant, we'd have to contextualise it for customers – as soon as the words 'creme caramel' exited your mouth, they'd be ordering it. It is such a special Mexican dessert – so simple, and yet never ever made vegan. Shannon has managed to perfectly and almost scientifically resolve this so you have the best, firmest, perfectly spiced and textured flan possible. Don't be daunted – just follow the guide and you'll know what flan is all about.

Serves 4–6

750 ml (25½ fl oz/3 cups) soy milk

1½ teaspoons vanilla extract or paste

4 cloves

6 fennel seeds

1 cinnamon stick

2 strips of orange peel, white pith removed

50 g (1¾ oz) caster (superfine) sugar

1 thyme sprig

pinch of salt

¾ teaspoon agar powder – no more, no less. I'm serious, this is not a time to be a cowboy

170 g (6 oz) silken tofu

Caramel

170 g (6 oz/¾ cup) caster (superfine) sugar

pinch of salt

You can either make 1 large flan, or 4–6 individual servings.

Place all of the ingredients except the tofu and agar in a medium-sized saucepan. Bring to the boil, then remove from the heat and transfer to a heatproof bowl. Set aside for the flavours to develop for 30 minutes. Wipe the saucepan clean for later use.

To make the caramel, combine the sugar, salt and 60 ml (2 fl oz/¼ cup) water in a very clean, small saucepan over medium heat, without stirring, until the sugar dissolves. Continue to cook until the liquid begins to turn a light amber, approximately 8–10 minutes. At this stage, don't walk away from the caramel because it WILL turn on you the very first chance it gets! Once the caramel resembles the piece of amber that holds the mosquito in *Jurassic Park*, you know you're good to go. Pour the caramel into your desired moulds and set aside while you finish the custard. Don't stress, the caramel will go hard.

Using a fine-meshed sieve, strain the infused soy milk back into the clean saucepan and sprinkle over the agar powder. Bring the mixture to the boil over medium heat, then reduce to a low simmer and stir for about 3 minutes to make sure the agar is fully dissolved. Set aside to cool a little.

Place the tofu in a blender and pour over the soy milk mixture. Blend well ensuring that you have no lumps. If you want to be extra sure that you have a totally smooth custard, pour the mixture through a fine-meshed sieve into a bowl. If you find that the blender has created a foam on top of the milk and you would rather the bottom of the flan to have a flat, smooth edge, feel free to spoon it off the surface if it bothers you. (We do this at the restaurant, but when Shannon's making this at home, she doesn't bother.) Pour the custard over the set caramel and cover with plastic wrap.

Set aside in the fridge for at least 2 hours to chill completely. To remove the flan from the mould, place in a sink or bowl of hot water for about 15 seconds to help soften the caramel, making sure you don't get any water on the flan. Place your serving dish on top, then quickly turn over allowing the flan to drop onto the dish. Don't be scared, it's easier than it sounds!

WARM MEXICAN CORN & BLUEBERRY PUDDINGS

Using corn chips in a crumble – let's just put it down to Shannon's weirdo brain. Sometimes, you can't question the ingenuity, especially when it tastes this good. These puddings are extra great served with a scoop of vanilla ice cream.

Preheat the oven to 170°C (340°F).

To make the puddings place the flour, polenta, salt, both sugars and baking powder in the bowl of a stand mixer with a paddle attachment and mix for 10 seconds to evenly blend the ingredients.

Put the soy milk, both oils, vanilla and the lemon zest and juice in a jug and stir to combine.

With the motor running on low speed, pour in the wet ingredients then turn up to a medium speed and mix for 1 minute. Fold through the blueberries.

To make the topping, combine the blueberries, cornflour and caster sugar in a bowl and toss the mixture until the blueberries are well coated.

Spray a large 6-hole muffin tin with olive oil spray and place a small circle of baking paper in the base of each hole. Spoon a little of the blueberry topping into each hole then top with 2 tablespoons of the muffin mixture. You can make smaller/more muffins if you prefer – just reduce the number of blueberries in the bottom slightly and adjust the cooking time.

Bake in the oven for 25–30 minutes or until a skewer inserted into the centre of a muffin comes out clean.

Meanwhile, to make the corn chip crumble, place all of the ingredients in a mixing bowl and rub the mixture through your hands until everything is coated in the melted butter and well combined. Spread the mixture evenly onto a baking tray and bake for 20 minutes or until golden brown. Set aside to cool to room temperature, then break it into crumble-sized pieces, although keep the texture a little rough.

To make the blueberry and lemon sauce, place all of the ingredients in a small saucepan and bring to a gentle simmer. Cook until the sugar is dissolved, then pour into a blender and blend until smooth.

Once the muffins are cooked, remove from the oven and place a chopping board or tray on top of the muffin tin, gently pressing down to flatten the cakes. Allow the muffins to cool for 5 minutes in the tin before inverting onto a wire rack.

Spoon a little of the sauce onto the base of each serving plate and place a pudding on top. Drizzle with a little extra sauce, then scatter the crumble mix over the plates.

Serves 4–6

Puddings

300 g (10½ oz/2 cups) plain (all-purpose) flour

110 g (4 oz/¾ cup) fine polenta (cornmeal)

1 teaspoon salt

165 g (5½ oz/¾ cup) brown sugar

170 g (6 oz/¾ cup) caster (superfine) sugar

1½ teaspoons baking powder

250 ml (8½ fl oz/1 cup) soy milk

60 ml (2 fl oz/¼ cup) vegetable oil

60 ml (2 fl oz/¼ cup) olive oil

1 teaspoon vanilla essence

zest and juice of 1 lemon

150 g (5½ oz) blueberries, fresh or frozen

olive oil spray

Blueberry Topping

150 g (5½ oz) blueberries, fresh or frozen

2 tablespoons cornflour (cornstarch)

2 tablespoons caster (superfine) sugar

Corn Chip Crumble

2–3 corn chips, crumbled

3 tablespoons polenta (cornmeal)

65 g (2 oz/¾ cup) desiccated (shredded) coconut

2 tablespoons brown sugar

pinch of ground cinnamon

2 tablespoons plain (all-purpose) flour

pinch of salt

2 tablespoons melted butter

Blueberry & Lemon Sauce

155 g (5½ oz) blueberries, fresh or frozen

110 g (4 oz/½ cup) caster (superfine) sugar

¼ teaspoon ground cinnamon

juice and zest of 1 lemon

½ teaspoon vanilla essence

WARM SPANISH DOUGHNUTS

Rejoice! The doughnut recipe! Shannon's got many a doughnut recipe up her sleeve, but these are everyone's favourite restaurant doughnuts.

Serves 4–6

1½ teaspoons active dried yeast

125 ml (4 fl oz/½ cup) warm water

pinch of sugar

550 g (1 lb 3 oz/3⅔ cups) plain (all-purpose) flour, plus extra for dusting

pinch of salt

1 teaspoon mixed spice

145 g (5 oz) caster (superfine) sugar

2 teaspoons no egg powder

250 ml (8½ fl oz/1 cup) warm soy milk (not hot!)

80 g (2¾ oz) butter

olive oil spray

vegetable oil, for deep-frying

cinnamon sugar for dusting, or your favourite doughnut coating

Filling ideas

Spanish quince paste

Chocolate Pâté (page 174)

Place the yeast, warm water and sugar in a small bowl and stir well to combine. Allow to sit for 5 minutes or until the mixture is bubbly.

Place the flour, salt, mixed spice, caster sugar and no egg powder in the bowl of a stand mixer with a dough hook attachment. Combine the yeast mixture with the warm soy milk and, with the stand mixer running on low speed, slowly pour the liquid into the dry ingredients. Continue to mix until the liquid is completely incorporated. If the mixture seems too sticky, add a little extra flour, 1 tablespoon at a time, until the dough begins to pull away from the side of the bowl.

Add half of the butter to the dough, increase the speed to medium and mix for 1 minute before adding the remaining butter. At this stage the dough may look like it doesn't want to take in the butter. If necessary, add a little extra flour again, 1 tablespoon at a time, until the dough just begins to pull away from the side of the bowl again. Knead on medium speed for around 4 minutes or until the dough is very soft, smooth and elastic. Place in a bowl that has been sprayed with olive oil and cover with plastic wrap. Set aside to prove in a warm place until doubled in size. This could take anywhere between 30–60 minutes depending on the temperature of the room.

Dust your work surface with flour and dump the dough on top. Dust a rolling pin with flour and roll out the dough until it is approximately 1.5 cm (½ in) thick. Cut out doughnuts using a round cookie cutter of any size, then transfer to a baking tray sprayed with olive oil. Cover loosely with plastic wrap and allow to prove again until the doughnuts have increased their size by half. The dough should feel very soft and bounce back slowly when pressed with your finger.

Heat enough oil for deep-frying in a deep-fryer or large heavy-based saucepan to 170°C (340°F) or until a scrap of dough dropped into the oil turns golden in 15 seconds. Carefully drop a few doughnuts into the oil, making sure not to overcrowd the pan. Fry the doughnuts for approximately 1 minute before turning over and frying for a further 1 minute. Obviously, if you decide to make larger doughnuts the cooking time will be a little longer, so just go on the colour and make sure you have a beautiful golden brown on both sides. Test one by breaking it in half to make sure they are cooked through. Transfer to paper towel and allow to cool slightly.

This is the point where you can get creative and fill the doughnuts with whatever you like. At the restaurant we coat them in cinnamon sugar and fill them with Spanish quince paste that has been whipped with a little hot water to make it easier to use in a piping bag. But Shannon's favourite way to eat these is simply dusted in cinnamon sugar and dipped in chocolate pâté.

168

POACHED QUINCES

Poached quinces are perfection. We decided to put these beauties in the sweet section because they can be enjoyed as a lighter treat after any of the massive meals you're making with the help of this book. But in addition to these being served with our Horchata Rice Pudding (page 26), or even our Sangría Crumble (page 173), you can and should eat them for brekkie or a snack on their own! Mmm quince snacks.

Place the quince in a bowl of cold water with a squeeze of lemon juice to prevent them browning. Set aside.

To make the poaching syrup, combine the remaining ingredients with 1 litre (34 fl oz/4 cups) water in a large heavy-based saucepan. Bring to the boil, stirring, until the sugar is dissolved.

Reduce the heat to the lowest simmer and add the quince wedges. Cover the quinces with a piece of baking paper and simmer for approximately 45 minutes, or until they can be pierced through easily with a knife. Make sure not to overcook or they will become mushy (which is fine if your goal is to make baby food – which it isn't so, don't. But hey, if you like softer, mushy, baby food-like fruit, that's your prerogative).

Remove from the heat and leave the quince wedges to sit in the syrup for 30 minutes to allow the flavours to develop and the colour to darken a little.

Strain the quince and keep the syrup for an added bonus to whatever dish you're serving the quinces with.

Serves 4–6

2 large quinces, peeled, cored and each cut into 6 wedges

3 lemon slices, plus the juice of ½ lemon

3 orange slices

2 cinnamon sticks

1 star anise

4 cloves

1 fresh bay leaf

4 whole peppercorns

345 g (12 oz/1½ cups) raw caster (superfine) or regular sugar

SANGRÍA CRUMBLE

When we first introduced this dish to the menu, we were going to use plums but they were about to go out of season. Pears were the seasonal solution. Really, when making this, use any fruit that's in right now and affordable: plums, quinces, pears, apples, anything that's your favourite. It's awesome served with saffron custard or your favourite vanilla ice cream.

Preheat the oven to 170°C (340°F).

Place 125 ml (4 fl oz/½ cup) water and all of the filling ingredients except the pears in a medium-sized saucepan and bring to the boil. Stir until the sugar is dissolved, then remove from the heat and allow to sit for at least 15 minutes for all the flavours to infuse.

To prepare the pears, cut off both ends and peel. Cut into quarters, then remove the core by cutting around the seeds. Place the cut pears in an ovenproof dish that is large enough to fit the pears in a single layer (it's fine if a few are resting on top of each other). Pour over the infused wine and cover the pears with some baking paper, pressing the paper down onto the surface. This will be easier to do if you cut the paper roughly the same size as the opening of the dish (if you wanna get fancy, the cheffy word for this is a cartouche).

Poach the pears in the oven for approximately 45 minutes or until a knife slips through the flesh without too much resistance. You don't want mush though (unless mush is your thing). Once the pears are cooked, remove from the poaching liquid and set aside in a bowl. Pour the poaching liquid into a saucepan and simmer over medium heat until the liquid has reduced by half and is beginning to look a little syrupy. Remove from the heat and set aside.

To make the crumble, combine all of the ingredients except the butter and flaked almonds in a bowl and mix well. Add the butter to the bowl and rub it into the dry mixture using your fingertips, until it resembles rough breadcrumbs with chunky bits through it. Gently stir through the flaked almonds.

Place a layer of pears on the bottom of an ovenproof dish or individual ceramic moulds, then cover with the crumble mixture. Now personally, I like a 50/50 fruit to crumble ratio, cos let's face it, the crumble is the best part! Very lightly press down on the crumble mixture to make sure it's filled any gaps between the pears. Make sure not to press too firmly though as you still want it to be a bit rough and bumpy. Bake for 25 minutes or until the top is golden and the juices from the fruit are beginning to bubble up around the edges.

To make the saffron custard, place all of the ingredients except the cornflour mixture in a medium-sized saucepan and bring to the boil. Remove from the heat and set aside to infuse for 15 minutes.

Remove the cinnamon stick, peel and cloves then return to a low heat. Pour the cornflour mixture into the infused soy milk and whisk until it begins to thicken, about 2 minutes. Serve warm with the crumble.

Serves 4–6

Filling

375 ml (12½ fl oz/1½ cups) red wine, any variety

125 ml (4 fl oz/½ cup) Pedro Xímenez sherry (or brandy works, too)

5 cloves

2 cinnamon sticks

4 black peppercorns

1 fresh bay leaf

2 star anise

peel of ½ orange, white pith removed, cut into strips

peel of ½ lemon, white pith removed, cut into strips

115 g (4 oz/½ cup) brown sugar

1.5 kg (3 lb 5 oz) pears

Crumble

100 g (3½ oz/1 cup) ground almonds

225 g (8 oz/1½ cups) plain (all-purpose) flour

2 teaspoons baking powder

pinch of salt

115 g (4 oz/½ cup) caster (superfine) sugar

115 g (4 oz/½ cup) brown sugar

1 teaspoon finely chopped rosemary leaves

1 teaspoon mixed spice

zest of ½ orange

185 g (6½ oz) cold butter

45 g (1¾ oz/½ cup) flaked almonds

Saffron Custard

500 ml (17 fl oz/2 cups) soy milk

2 strips orange peel, white pith
removed

1 cinnamon stick

1 teaspoon vanilla bean paste
or extract

pinch of saffron threads

2 whole cloves

55 g (2 oz/¼ cup) caster (superfine)
sugar

3 teaspoons cornflour (cornstarch)
mixed with 60 ml (2 fl oz/¼ cup)
soy milk

PAN CON CHOCOLATE

Chocolate Pâté

The origin of this dish comes from Shannon's childhood and her grandad. Shannon has great memories of her Puppy, her father's father, going to the Preston market and buying slabs of dark chocolate in bulk. Once home, he'd use a hammer to break the chocolate into bits and put it between bread with olive oil and salt and that would be lunch. He never made it into pâté, and Shannon didn't realise it was a Spanish thing. She just thought it a bit of an eccentric Puppy thing to do, but then, after cooking and travelling in Spain, she tasted the real deal and realised Puppy had obviously had it before and just made a weird ghetto Aussie version for her. It's really a shame he's not alive to see this book or recipe come to life. This one's for you, Puppy.

Serves 4–6

125 ml (4½ fl oz/½ cup) chickpea water (the juice that chickpeas share the tin with; strain the chickpeas and save them for another use)

pinch of citric acid

200 g (7 oz) caster (superfine) sugar

200 g (7 oz) dark chocolate (at least 60% cacao)

50 g (1¾ oz) butter

½ teaspoon ground cinnamon

Garnish

fennel seed baguette or regular baguette, sliced and toasted (optional)

strong-flavoured extra-virgin olive oil

sea salt flakes

fennel seeds, toasted and crushed (optional)

Place the chickpea water and citric acid in the bowl of a stand mixer with a balloon whisk attachment and whisk until firm peaks form. This may take up to 5 minutes, so be patient. Slowly add the sugar in a steady stream and whisk until the meringue mixture becomes stiff and glossy.

There are two ways you can melt the chocolate: either place in a microwave-safe bowl and heat at 10 second intervals until melted; or put the chocolate in a bowl and set it over a saucepan of simmering water and stir until melted. Don't let the bottom of the bowl touch the water in the saucepan. Once fully melted, add the butter and cinnamon and stir well to combine.

Using a spatula or metal spoon, gently fold the melted chocolate through the meringue until evenly mixed through, then pour into individual ramekins or a large serving dish. Set aside in the fridge for at least 1 hour until set.

Serve the pâté with a side of toasted bread and drizzle with a strong extra-virgin olive oil and sea salt flakes. At Smith & Daughters, we use a beautiful fennel seed baguette, which goes really well with the chocolate, so feel free to sprinkle a little toasted crushed fennel seeds over the pâté along with the salt.

174

DRINKS

When we conceived Smith & Daughters, we wanted to design the drinks around the food. To have a place where you could have an awesome meal and drinks to match is a rarity in the vegan community, so we strived to make that environment. Here, you have a collection of our very best and most popular drinks from all our menus. They're perfectly balanced, sweet, savoury, sour, and there's a little something for everyone, even the non-drinkers.

SPLASH OF LASH

Lash is one of our original bar staff members. Lash is definitely a refreshing addition to the human race, so we thought why not name this drink after him?! It's perfect, and even though he still blushes anytime anyone mentions it, he knows how much we love him. This is by far our most beloved mocktail. So much so that we upgraded it to include vodka if our patrons so choose.

Makes 1

4 watermelon or pineapple wedges, cut into 2 cm (¾ in) squares

2 lime wedges, cut into 4 pieces

small handful mint, plus 1 mint sprig, for garnish (optional)

ice cubes

sweet coconut water

Muddle the fruit in a tall glass. Crush the mint with your hands and place on top of the fruit. Fill the glass with ice, then pour over enough coconut water to come to the top. Use a bar spoon to bring up the fruit from the bottom of the glass and to evenly disperse the bits.

Garnish with a sprig of mint, if desired.

TROPICAL

CHESTER'S
REALITY

UP & MO

LOVELY BERRY

CHESTER'S REALITY SMOOTHIE

Chester came to us and didn't say two words the first time he met us. He was an unassuming and meek Welshman, but came highly skilled and recommended. His résumé listed that he was a former Sea Shepherd engineer, ER nurse, sailor, computer tech, and *Jurassic Park* mega-fan. We knew there was something there, so we hired him as a food runner. Within weeks he escalated to waiter, bartender, barista and (unofficial title) weekend brunch drinks manager. He trained staff, fixed everything, took inventory, kept the peace, and was, generally, the best. The most hilarious title he held was best straight-edge bartender in our suburb – he didn't drink the drinks, but he made them perfectly every time. He now manages our vegan deli, Smith & Deli, and we love him very much.

Makes 1

1 tablespoon cacao butter

splash of hot water

2 tablespoons coconut oil

2 bananas, roughly chopped, plus 1 banana slice, for garnish (optional)

60 ml (2 fl oz/¼ cup) coconut milk

2 teaspoons cocoa powder, plus extra, to serve (optional)

1 teaspoon maca powder (optional)

drizzle of agave syrup, to taste

60 ml (2 fl oz/¼ cup) coffee, plus coffee beans, for garnish (optional)

250 ml (8½ fl oz/1 cup) almond milk

large handful ice cubes

Place the cacao butter and a splash of hot water in a blender and blitz until smooth. Add the coconut oil, banana and coconut milk, and blend. Add the cocoa powder, maca powder (if using), agave, coffee and almond milk, and blend again. Finally, add the ice and give it one more blitz.

Pour into a small glass and garnish with a slice of banana, a dusting of cocoa powder and coffee beans, if desired.

TROPICAL SMOOTHIE

Why not make everything in your life a summery paradise? Go full troppo with your morning smoothie. We like to think passionfruit makes everything better.

Makes 1

2 tablespoons cacao butter

splash of hot water

1 tablespoon coconut oil

½ banana, sliced

splash of coconut cream

splash of almond milk

splash of agave syrup

¼ mango

2 tablespoons passionfruit pulp, plus 1 teaspoon extra, to serve (optional)

½ orange, peeled

4 ice cubes

Place the cacao butter and a splash of hot water in a blender and blend until melted. Add the coconut oil, banana, coconut cream, almond milk and agave and blend again. Add the remaining ingredients except the ice cubes and give it another blitz.

Taste and adjust the flavouring, if necessary, then add the ice cubes and blend a final time.

Pour into a highball glass and garnish with the extra passionfruit pulp, if desired.

LOVELY BERRY SMOOTHIE

Berry delicious. Berry lovely.

Makes 1

1½ tablespoons coconut oil

150 ml (5 fl oz) almond milk

2 tablespoons agave syrup

2 tablespoons blueberries, plus 1 extra blueberry, sliced, for garnish (optional)

2 tablespoons raspberries

2 tablespoons strawberries, plus 1 extra strawberry, sliced, for garnish (optional)

75 ml (2½ fl oz) coconut kefir

100 ml (3½ fl oz) coconut cream

½ banana, sliced

Place the coconut oil, almond milk and agave in a blender and blend until smooth. Add the remaining ingredients and blend again.

Pour into a highball glass and garnish with the sliced blueberry and strawberry, if desired.

UP & MO

This is what Mo should be drinking in the morning instead of her typical breakfast of nothing.

Makes 1

1 banana

4 tablespoons muesli

3 teaspoons maple syrup, plus extra to garnish (optional)

250 ml (8½ fl oz/1 cup) almond milk

dash of chai tea syrup

4 ice cubes

oats, to garnish (optional)

cinnamon sticks, to garnish (optional)

Place all of the ingredients in a blender and blend until smooth.

Serve in a small glass, and garnish with the oats, cinnamon sticks and maple syrup, if desired.

HORCHATA

Horchata is such a classic Spanish and Mexican drink we had to include it in so many ways at Smith & Daughters. And we thought why not mix it up? In Mexico, horchata is typically made with rice, but in Spain they use almonds, so we used both! We started with the basic horchata, which over ice and topped with cinnamon is a dream, but then made it into a Rice Pudding (page 26) deeeelish, and then added cognac, espresso and a few other things and made a crazy popular cocktail (see below). What can't horchata do?

Makes 1 litre (34 fl oz/4 cups)

200 g (7 oz/1 cup) jasmine rice or long-grain rice

80 g (2¾ oz/½ cup) almonds, with or without skins

750 ml (25½ fl oz/3 cups) hot water

½ teaspoon ground cinnamon, plus extra, for garnish (optional)

2 cloves

2 strips of orange peel, white pith removed

230 g (8 oz/1 cup) caster (superfine) sugar

1 teaspoon vanilla bean paste or extract

pinch of salt

ice cubes

Place the rice, almonds and hot water in a blender. Blend on low speed for 10 seconds. Add the ground cinnamon, cloves and orange peel. Set aside for at least 4 hours or, preferably, overnight.

Remove the orange peel and blend the rice and almond mixture again, but this time blend until the mixture is as smooth as possible. Add 1 litre (34 fl oz/4 cups) water along with the sugar, vanilla and salt and blend again until well combined.

Line a fine-meshed sieve with a few layers of muslin (cheesecloth) and set it over a large bowl. Pour the horchata into the sieve, about 250 ml (8½ fl oz/1 cup) at a time, pushing onto the solids to get as much liquid as possible.

Pour the horchata into a jug. If you prefer a slightly thinner horchata, add another 250 ml (8½ fl oz/1 cup) water and stir to combine.

Serve chilled over ice and dusted with cinnamon, if desired.

GANGSTER HORCHATA

Makes 1

45 ml (1¾ fl oz) cognac (at the restaurant, we use Martell VS Cognac)

30 ml (1 fl oz) Horchata (see above)

30 ml (1 fl oz) espresso, plus 3 coffee beans, for garnish (optional)

1½ teaspoons triple sec

4 dashes of bitters

2 teaspoons simple syrup

ice cubes

lemon twist, for garnish (optional)

ground cinnamon, for garnish (optional)

Simple syrup (see note)

220 g (8 oz/1 cup) sugar

To make the simple syrup, place the sugar and 250 ml (8½ fl oz/1 cup) water in a small saucepan and bring to the boil. Reduce the heat to low and simmer until the sugar is completely dissolved. Set aside to cool, then pour into a glass bottle.

Add the cognac, horchata, espresso, triple sec, bitters and syrup to a cocktail shaker, then fill with ice and shake.

Single strain into a chilled rocks glass filled with ice.

Garnish with a classic lemon twist, 3 coffee beans and dust with cinnamon, if desired.

Note: This is a 50/50 recipe, so if you don't need this much, feel free to make less or more, as long as your measurements are equal.

PINK LEMONADE

If drinking this refreshing and very pink lemonade, you should probably go big. Break out your best glass jug – quadruple the recipe, bring some friends around (or don't) and find a nice porch to sit on. Not too sweet, very, very easy to drink and just a little bit different with the bonus of thyme and elderflower.

Makes 1

45 ml (1½ fl oz) strawberry purée (blended to be on the chunky side)

30 ml (1 fl oz) vodka

15 ml (½ fl oz) lemon juice, plus a few thin lemon slices

leaves from 1 thyme sprig, plus extra sprigs, for garnish (optional)

15 ml (½ fl oz) St Germain elderflower liqueur

ice cubes

lemon soda

lemon spiral, for garnish (optional)

Build everything except the lemon soda in a highball glass, stirring constantly.

Top with lemon soda and stir.

Garnish with a lemon spiral and sprigs of thyme, if desired.

EL NIÑO

We have yet to find someone who doesn't second order our take on the classic tiki-style Dark & Stormy cocktail. We love a good dark rum, lime & mint combo, but when you add tamarind paste, tamarind soda, and fresh ginger, people are reeling for more. It's all about keeping the drinkers guessing and adding those complementary flavours that you wonder why you hadn't thought of it sooner yourself! Can I get another?

Makes 1

8 mint leaves, plus 1 mint sprig, for garnish (optional)

2 slices ginger, finely chopped

45 ml (1½ fl oz) spiced rum

2 barspoons tamarind syrup

2 barspoons agave syrup

30 ml (1 fl oz) lime juice

ice cubes

tamarind soda

Muddle the mint and ginger in a tall glass. Add the spiced rum, tamarind syrup, agave and lime juice, then fill with ice and shake. Pour into a highball glass and top with tamarind soda.

Garnish with a mint sprig, if desired.

JALAPEÑO CUCUMBER CORIANDER MARGARITA

This delicious cocktail is worth a special mention as it's our signature drink. It's everything you want in a margarita and more – refreshing, spicy, savoury, sweet – and it even makes you enjoy tequila. We have numerous tequila converts based on this drink alone.

Makes 1

chilli salt

small handful roughly diced cucumber, plus an elongated slice, for garnish (optional)

3 coriander (cilantro) sprigs

3 slices jalapeño, plus extra, for garnish (optional)

50 ml (1¾ fl oz) tequila blanco (at the restaurant we use Tromba Blanco)

20 ml (¾ fl oz) agave syrup

30 ml (1 fl oz) lime juice

ice cubes

Dip the moistened rim of a martini glass in chilli salt until well coated.

Muddle the cucumber, coriander and jalapeño in a cocktail shaker. Add the tequila, agave and lime juice, then fill with ice and shake hard for a minimum of 10 seconds.

Double strain into the martini glass and serve garnished with the slice of cucumber and jalapeño, if desired.

Note: Chilli salt can be found at any Latin supermarket, or you can simply use salt.

CANTALOUPE & CHIPOTLE MARGARITA

Being a Latin restaurant we always challenge ourselves to come up with interesting and refreshing margarita flavours. The sweetness of the cantaloupe and the smoky spiciness of the chipotle achieves just that.

Makes 1

salt

small handful roughly diced rockmelon (cantaloupe), plus a small wedge, for garnish (optional)

1 teaspoon chipotle in adobo

45 ml (1½ fl oz) tequila blanco (at the restaurant we use Tromba Blanco)

15 ml (½ fl oz) lime juice

ice cubes

Dip the moistened rim of a martini glass in salt until well coated.

Muddle the melon and chipotle in a cocktail shaker. Add the remaining ingredients, then fill with ice and shake.

Double strain into the prepared martini glass and garnish with a wedge of melon, if desired.

BLOOD ORANGE & BASIL MARGARITA

Bloody oranges, at it again, making incredible combos with tequila and basil. This margarita is particularly amazing on the rocks with salt.

Makes 1

salt

50 ml (1¾ fl oz) blanco tequila (at the restaurant we use Tromba Blanco)

4 basil leaves, plus extra, for garnish (optional)

25 ml (¾ fl oz) lemon juice

30 ml (1 fl oz) blood orange juice

15 ml (½ fl oz) agave syrup

ice cubes

Dip the moistened rim of a martini glass in salt until well coated.

Muddle the basil in a cocktail shaker. Add the remaining ingredients, then fill with ice and shake.

Double strain into the prepared martini glass and garnish with a basil leaf, if desired.

SIESTA

No competition, at the top of the list for most beloved cocktail by staff. Mezcal, when used properly, makes alcoholic magic.

Makes 1

60 ml (2 fl oz/¼ cup) mezcal

45 ml (1½ fl oz) lemon juice

15 ml (½ fl oz) St Germain elderflower liqueur

15 ml (½ fl oz) thyme syrup

ice cubes

lemon twist, for garnish (optional)

Thyme syrup

220 g (8 oz/1 cup) sugar

3 thyme sprigs, plus extra, for garnish (optional)

To make the thyme syrup, place the sugar, thyme and 250 ml (8½ fl oz/1 cup) water in a small saucepan and bring to the boil. Reduce the heat to low and simmer until the sugar is completely dissolved. Set aside to cool, then pour into a glass bottle, leaving the thyme in the syrup to infuse. The longer you leave it, the stronger the flavour will be.

Add all of the ingredients to a cocktail shaker, then fill with ice and shake. Double strain into a short glass.

Garnish with a classic lemon twist and a sprig of thyme, if desired.

SLOE BERRY SOUR

This sour was often neck-and-neck with the Jalapeño Margarita for popularity. A blend of citrus, blueberries and everyone's favourite Sloe Gin makes for a very drinkable, lovely treat.

Makes 1

2 barspoons of blueberries, plus a small skewer of blueberries, for garnish (optional)

30 ml (1 fl oz) sloe gin

15 ml (½ fl oz) gin (at the restaurant we use Beefeater)

15 ml (½ fl oz) triple sec

20 ml (¾ fl oz) lemon juice

15 ml (½ fl oz) grapefruit juice

20 ml (¾ fl oz) orange juice, plus an orange twist, for garnish (optional)

ice cubes

Muddle the blueberries in a cocktail shaker. Add the remaining ingredients, then fill with ice and shake hard for a minimum of 10 seconds.

Double strain into a chilled rocks glass filled with ice and garnish with a skewer of blueberries and a twist of orange, if desired.

BASIL LUCHADOR

Like a swift delicious punch to the face by a Mexican fighter, the luchador. It's simple, really: basil, lemon and gin. No need for anything more.

Makes 1

handful basil leaves, plus extra, for garnish (optional)

juice of ½ lemon

60 ml (2 fl oz/¼ cup) gin

20 ml (¾ fl oz) Simple Syrup (page 185)

ice

Muddle the basil and lemon juice in a cocktail shaker. Add the gin and syrup, then fill with ice and shake. Double strain over ice into a rocks glass.

Garnish with a basil leaf, if desired.

SMOKY GONZALES

Ol' smoky was and still is one of the house favourites. Some people love chocolate and orange, but we love smoky oranges – it's gives a margarita the sophistication it deserves. Go Smoky Gonzales go. Arriba! Arriba! Andale! Arriba!

Makes 1

chilli salt (see note)

ice cubes

45 ml (1½ fl oz) mezcal (the smokier, the better)

15 ml (½ fl oz) orange curaçao

15 ml (½ fl oz) lime juice

15 ml (½ fl oz) fresh orange juice, plus an orange wheel, for garnish (optional)

2 teaspoons agave syrup

Half-rim a rocks glass with chilli salt and fill with ice.

Combine the remaining ingredients in a cocktail shaker, then fill with ice and shake hard.

Strain into the prepared glass and garnish with an orange wheel, if desired.

Note: Chilli salt can be found at any Latin supermarket, or you can simply use salt.

BITTER JESS

Bitter Jess is created by and named after Jess, our epically talented bar manager, who'd like for you to think she's bitter, but really she's a big softy and very kind on the inside. Come visit and let her make you an outstanding cocktail.

Makes 1

45 ml (1¾ fl oz) Aperol

30 ml (1 fl oz) St Germain elderflower liqueur

30 ml (1 fl oz) lime juice, plus a lime wheel, for garnish (optional)

1 mango cheek

ice cubes

orange peel, for garnish (optional)

Throw the Aperol, elderflower liqueur, lime juice and mango cheek in a blender and blitz briefly. Add a large handful of ice and blitz again. Pour into a tall glass.

Garnish with a lime wheel and some orange peel, if desired. Also, use a wide straw as this is quite slushy-like in texture.

OLD CUBAN

One of our most popular cocktails in the summer time. What you love about a mojito and a mule, all topped with sparkling. Can't go wrong.

Makes 1

6–8 mint leaves, plus extra sprigs, for garnish (optional)

45 ml (1¾ fl oz) dark rum

15 ml (½ fl oz) lime juice, plus a lime wheel, for garnish (optional)

15 ml (½ fl oz) Simple Syrup (page 185)

2 dashes of bitters

ice

60 ml (2 fl oz/¼ cup) sparkling wine

Half-fill a stemless wine glass with ice.

Muddle the mint leaves in a cocktail shaker. Add the rum, lime juice, syrup and bitters, then fill with ice and shake.

Single strain into the chilled wine glass and top with the sparkling wine. Garnish with some extra mint and a lime wheel, if desired.

PIÑA COLADA

If you like… delicious tropical beverages, and getting caught by a… barbecue, this drink is so perfect for you. With an emphasis on using whole, fresh ingredients, our Piña Colada is super special because it calls for fresh pineapple that we chargrill and real coconut flesh for taste and texture. Anyone can put some Malibu, bottled pineapple juice and coconut cream together, but this is taking it to the next level. Step it up, Piña Colada.

Preheat the oven to 180°C (350°F).

Heat a chargrill pan over high heat and cook 4 pineapple wedges until char marks appear. Remove from the heat and set aside.

Place the coconut flakes on a baking tray lined with baking paper and toast in the oven for about 7 minutes, checking often to ensure that they don't burn. Set aside to cool.

Dip the rim of a highball glass in agave syrup, then coat with the toasted coconut flakes.

Place the grilled pineapple and remaining ingredients in a blender and blend until slushy. Pour everything into the prepared glass.

Garnish with the remaining fresh pineapple wedge and 2 pineapple fronds, if desired.

Makes 1

5 pineapple wedges, plus 2 fronds, for garnish (optional)

handful coconut flakes

agave syrup

30 ml (1 fl oz) sweet coconut water

30 ml (1 fl oz) white rum

30 ml (1 fl oz) coconut rum

15 ml (½ fl oz) Simple Syrup (page 185), made with brown sugar

15 ml (½ fl oz) lime juice

3 strips of coconut flesh

1 dash of bitters (seriously, just one – no pink drinks)

1½ large handfuls ice cubes

197

INDEX

201

202

ACKNOWLEDGEMENTS

Shannon would like to thank:

Mum and Richard, Antoni, Jayden, Beccie and Noelie, Dad, Grandma and Puppy, Maisen, D, Mo and Callum, all my kitchen staff who let me do things in my own 'special way' and put up with it.

Mo would like to thank:

Mom and Dad, Grams and Pops, Rae and Sam, Casey and Ashley, Callum, Shannon, Maisen, Marilyn, Robert, Heath, Sarah, Charlotte, Ruby, Danielle, Matt, Stella, Ollie, Greg Bennick, Alice and RoRo, Emillie and Lloyd, Tabby and EJ, Leslie Knope, Colette, Marina, Ashley, Danielle Corns, Bronwyn, Hannah, Steven, Lily Jane and Millie, Heather, Jason and Brandie Bailey, Beth Gould, Sue Turner, Jade and Jason Wong, Dan Piraro and allllll the other unnamed people who made me the big, thankful maniac I am today.

Both of us would like to thank:

Designer, builder, fixer, photographer, everyman: Callum Preston

Our management team: Tracey Savio, Alice Blackburne, Jessica Ladha, Chester Bie, Lara Mihan and Jessica Schiffke

The rest of our crew: Holly Rattray, Vinnie Allen, Tamara Scoulidis, Tom Hogan, Hannah Johnstone, Emma James, Selina Ruane, Hana Davies, Rachel Johnstone, Leah Evans, Nick Megchelse, Zian Reyne, Gabby Galletly, Sarah Watters, Mark Santo Domingo, Dan McKay, Aaron Faruggia, Dan Teague, Jack Forbes, Alana Musolino, Deb Hurst, Jerome Scaffidi, Tony Bracey, Milena Zuccarello, Luke Chang, Liam Clapp, Tash Iodice, Dean Hurlihy.

And all past and future teams: thanks for shaping us into the place we are now.

Our Hardie Grant team, especially: Jane Willson, Meelee Soorkia, Vaughan Mossop, Bonnie Savage, Leesa O'Reilly, Lucy Heaver, Roxy Ryan

Hair: Sam Castoro

Makeup and hair: Hannah Marshall

Personal trainer/posi mentor: Roy Hanford

Photography: Benn Wood, Nicole Reed, Callum Preston, Bonnie Savage, Nicole Goodwin

Fruit and veg: The Vegetable Connection

PR: Luke McKinnon

Our customers

Our friends

Everyone who's supported us along the way and continues to believe in what we do.

ABOUT THE AUTHORS

MO WYSE

Things to know about Mo:

She's short. She's mighty. She loves her family and friends and working. She believes in Positive Mental Attitude. She LOVES FOOD (and working). And owning Smith & Daughters. And being a part of this little growing empire is the best, hardest, most rewarding thing she's ever done.

Born in Seattle, USA, Mo was a classic over-achiever nerd who fell into the punk and hardcore scene at an early age. She went to a Catholic all-girls school and attended Jewish community-centre summer-camp programs, where she was a camp counsellor. She loved everything, did sports, was a drama and choir geek, became student body president and went vegan on her 16th birthday.

She got a scholarship and moved to New York a week after graduating high school. She studied journalism and historical media studies at New York University, worked for an environmentalism/social justice/animal advocacy magazine, *Satya*, waited tables at popular New York veg restaurant Red Bamboo, lived in Brooklyn with her best friends, got a lot of arguably (not) regrettable tattoos, rode bikes, rescued cats, promoted veganism all over the city, learned some independent business ropes by working PR and marketing for a friend's business, Vegan Treats, and became PA to renowned cartoonist Dan Piraro.

Then she got roped back into working for the family's business by her own father. Ed Wyse Beauty Supplies, est. 1956 was needing an (essentially) youthful revivalist, so Mo moved back to Seattle. Her first assignment: go to Australia to learn everything about a product line based in Melbourne. First stop in Australia: fall in love with her now husband, Callum Preston. Working through a long-distance relationship and repping the family company, the ball had to drop. The company sponsored Callum to live in the USA for two years. At the end of the stay, they decided to give Melbourne a go. Not a day into being here, Mo was itching for a job and replied to an ad on Gumtree for an events coordinator for an outdoor summer project, The People's Market, and the rest is Mo/Shannon history. In the period before finding 175 Brunswick Street to house Smith & Daughters, Mo freelanced as a production assistant for Mercedes Benz Fashion Week Australia and *The Ellen Show*, and became a questions producer for Channel 7's *Million Dollar Minute*.

Talk about a crazy history. Thankfully, it all ended in her greatest passions: food, and working ridiculous hours. Now ... world domination.

SHANNON MARTINEZ

Shannon was always where the food was. When her dad was cooking, she was helping. When the entire family was in the lounge room, she was in the kitchen with her grandmother, cooking. At school, her friends waited outside the classroom after home economics to eat Shannon's food.

Shannon's work history goes like this: 1995 – Ivanhoe Bakeshop, 15 years old making coffee and sandwiches; 1994–2000 – assisting her mum in her clothing shop; 1999 – dropping out of conventional school and re-entering doing an Advanced Certificate in Cookery. After an 8.30 am–3.30 pm school day, Shannon would catch the train into the city and work in the banquets kitchen at The Sofitel as one of two women in a team of thirty chefs. Her mum would pick her up at 9 pm. She did her required 48 hours to complete her certificate, stayed on and worked for free because she liked it so much. She got a job at Stephanie Alexander's Richmond Hill Larder and enrolled in the William Angliss Culinary Institute apprenticeship program. After three months she quit. The program didn't accept any of her Sofitel work. To this day, she admits to being a brat who should have stuck with it. She wanted to learn how to cook, but not like this.

The next seven years of Shannon's life was a mixed bag: married a professional skateboarder, swiftly divorced; worked heaps of exciting and strange bar jobs; played in bands; played the Vans Warped Tour; travelled the world. She did a brief stint at De Los Santos, ironically within the current location of Smith & Daughters, before working at The East Brunswick Club because the chef had to go to the 'bank' on a Friday and never came back. They knew she was a cook, not a chef, but they let her have full reign anyway. The epic Vegan Parma was created, and it started outselling the meaty one. The East sold the business, and the Gasometer Hotel in Collingwood opened. Shannon was asked to run the kitchen. As head chef she created some epic vegan and meaty menus for two years. Mo came along and while they were planning S&D, Shannon was appointed Head Chef at The Sweetwater Inn. She put them on the map for classic Aussie pub fare, with both meat and vegan menus.

Shannon attributes opening a restaurant to her mother's encouragement. The rest of her family was against it. Why would you work for yourself when you could be well paid and stress free and work for someone else? Her mum insisted – why would you work for someone else when you could be your own boss? She was the one to push the vegan card – if you open a mainstream restaurant, you're competing against hundreds, thousands. But vegans? None. This was the challenge, and Shannon never shies away from a challenge.

This edition published in 2022 by Hardie Grant Books,
an imprint of Hardie Grant Publishing
First published in 2016

Hardie Grant Books (Melbourne)
Wurundjeri Country
Building 1, 658 Church Street
Richmond, Victoria 3121

Hardie Grant Books (London)
5th & 6th Floors
52–54 Southwark Street
London SE1 1UN

hardiegrantbooks.com

Hardie Grant acknowledges the Traditional Owners of the country
on which we work, the Wurundjeri people of the Kulin nation and the
Gadigal people of the Eora nation, and recognises their continuing
connection to the land, waters and culture. We pay our respects to
their Elders past and present.

A catalogue record for this
book is available from the
National Library of Australia

Smith & Daughters
ISBN 978 1 74379 908 6

10 9 8 7 6 5 4 3 2 1

Publishing Director: Jane Willson/Michael Harry
Project Editor: Meelee Soorkia
Editor: Lucy Heaver
Design Manager: Vaughan Mossop/Kristin Thomas
Designers: Callum Preston/Vaughan Mossop
Photographer: Bonnie Savage
Stylist: Leesa O'Reilly
Production Manager: Todd Rechner
Production Coordinator: Jessica Harvie

Colour reproduction by Splitting Image Colour Studio
Printed in China by Leo Paper Products LTD.